Breakthrough to Meaning

Helping Your Kids Become Better Readers, Writers, and Thinkers

Jean Anne Clyde
Shelli Zechella Barber
Sandra Lynn Hogue
Laura Lynn Wasz

HEINEMANN
Portsmouth, NH

Heinemann
A division of Reed Elsevier Inc.
361 Hanover Street
Portsmouth, NH 03801–3912
www.heinemann.com

Offices and agents throughout the world

The authors and publisher wish to thank those who have generously given permission to reprint borrowed material:

Figure 1.1: *The Present* by William Edward West, 1833, oil on canvas. Bequest of Mrs. Blakemore Wheeler, No. 1964.31.33. Courtesy of The Speed Art Museum, Louisville, Kentucky.

Figures 1.2 and 1.3: From *Ruby the Copycat* by Peggy Rathmann. Copyright © 1991 by Margaret Rathmann. Reprinted by permission of Scholastic Inc.

Figure 6.2: Student practice materials from *Classroom Connections TERRANOVA.* Copyright © 2002 by CTB/McGraw-Hill LLC. Reprinted by permission of the McGraw-Hill Companies, Inc.

Figure 8.1: *Lewis and Clark on the Lower Columbia* by Charles M. Russell, 1905, opaque and transparent watercolor over graphite underdrawing on paper, No. 1961.195. Courtesy of the Amon Carter Museum, Fort Worth, Texas.

Library of Congress Cataloging-in-Publication Data
Breakthrough to meaning : helping your kids become better readers, writers, and thinkers / Jean Anne
    Clyde . . . [et al.].
        p. cm.
    Includes bibliographical references.
    ISBN-13: 978-0-325-00832-5
    ISBN-10: 0-325-00832-9
    1. Language arts (Elementary). 2. Subtext (Drama, novel, etc.). I. Clyde, Jean Anne.
    LB1576.B597 2006
    372.6—dc22   2006019999

Editor: Lois Bridges
Production editor: Sonja S. Chapman
Cover design: Night & Day Design
Compositor: Tom Allen/Pear Graphic Design
Manufacturing: Steve Bernier

Printed in the United States of America on acid-free paper
10 09 08 07 06 EB 1 2 3 4 5

Contents

For teachers everywhere, that they have the courage to embrace a teacher-researcher stance during these too political times. Their willingness to pursue answers to their own questions will keep them alive professionally and will surely make a difference for the kids whose lives they touch.

Foreword

The function of a foreword, like the function of curriculum, is to give perspective. One question I kept trying to answer as I was reading this book was, "How does what these authors are advocating fit within some larger conception of what a language arts program for the twenty-first century should look like?"

At first blush the book seems to be about a single strategy—the subtext strategy, not about curriculum at all. But this is misleading. First, these authors use the subtext strategy across the curriculum and in so doing demonstrate that unlike a "skill," which gets applied when the conditions are right (we add an "ed" to most verbs when we want to make them the past tense), a "strategy" refers to an underlying, fundamental process or set of processes in literacy. From what I can tell, the subtext strategy supports students in taking on for themselves the social practices of what it means to be critically literate. Across its various renditions—in reading, writing, inquiry, test-taking—it supports students in taking on a critical stance to the point where such a stance becomes second nature, "natural," if you will.

Elsewhere I have argued that "a good language arts program for the twenty-first century continues to be comprised of three components—meaning making, language study, and inquiry-based learning, *but* (and this is a big *but*) the emphasis is different" (Harste 2003, p. 8). That different emphasis, I went on to say, is critical literacy.

This book elaborates on this framework without necessarily meaning to. While the authors do not say that it is not enough to just emphasize "meaning making," they nonetheless demonstrate how the subtext strategy helps children unpack what they are reading so as to become consciously aware of systems of meaning that are operating in the text and how these systems of meaning position them and endow them with an identity they may or may not wish to take on. That's a big part of taking on a critical stance toward literacy.

Too often "language study" gets reduced to phonics in reading, and spelling and grammar in the area of writing. I argue that this has never been good enough, but even more so when it comes to preparing twenty-first-century literate beings. Children need to become text analysts, conscious of not only what the text is doing to readers, but also how it is doing this work. When used as a tool to support children in writing, the subtext strategy alerts children to how texts work. Children become agents of text rather than victims of text. That's another big part of what it means to develop a critical stance toward literacy.

The third component, "inquiry-based learning," references these authors' beliefs that curriculum needs to provide lots and lots of opportunities for students to explore their own inquiry questions using reading, writing, and other sign systems as tools and toys for learning. The goal, of course, is learning, a repositioning of oneself in the world both in terms of how one talks as well as how one acts. This, too, is what it means to take on a critical stance toward literacy.

Using meaning making, language study, and inquiry as a framework, what I found these authors advocating via the subtext strategy is the creation of critically literate beings who know the importance of: (1) being consciously aware of what others just take for granted, (2) entertaining multiple perspectives for purposes of growth, (3) taking on the responsibility to inquire and inform one's self, and who are (4) constantly repositioning themselves in the world in a more thoughtful and equitable manner.

Taken together, I see these four components as what is strategic about the subtext strategy. These are fundamental processes—fundamental social practices, if you will—in literacy. They define what it means to take on or to have developed "a critical stance." And, this is what makes the book curricular. In it the authors lay out how the use of the subtext strategy in its various renditions across the curriculum supports children in developing the kind of literacy needed for the twenty-first century.

While this, in itself, is a monumental feat, the book offers even more. There is, for example, something about a good teacher that simply takes my breath away. In this book there is not just one good teacher, but a whole study group all exploring a single strategy and how it might be varied to support students in becoming literate for the twenty-first century. The result is breathtaking. Not only does the reader understand what it means for students to take a critical stance toward literacy, but also what it means for teachers to take such a stance.

Teaching the English language arts is hard work. As our knowledge of literacy changes, so do the demands. Unfortunately, we teachers are always expected to be creating curriculum we never ourselves had the pleasure to experience firsthand. I would have loved to have been in a classroom where teachers were using the subtext strategy and in which they had set aside an extended period for literature discussion, another extended period for writing each day, and an hour or two in which I could explore a topic of my own choosing. I can only imagine what a different literate being I would be today had these been my experiences growing up.

Importantly, then, what we have here is a group of teachers imagining what might be. Their imagining is powerful. Not only do they teach us what it means for us, as teachers, to take on a critical stance relative to our teaching, but by sharing their imagining they give us a window on what our classrooms might be like as we, too, explore using the subtext strategy in our curricula. Now that is a perspective from which the whole profession can grow.

—Jerome C. Harste
Bloomington, IN
March 2006

Reference

Harste, J. C. 2003. What do we mean by literacy now? *Voices from the Middle*, 10 (3), 8–12.

Acknowledgments

First, huge thanks to J. Daniel Herring who provided the initial experience with dramatic literacy that set our research into motion. His inspiration and insight have been invaluable.

To Jerry Harste, for the carefully crafted foreword that frames this book. His work has provided a foundation upon which this research has been built.

To Lyla, Wyatt, and Seth, our collective children, for caring for themselves and one another, and for understanding when we had to work yet another weekend on this project that has so filled our lives for the past year. Memories of their wonderful play—with water hoses, balloons, and other everyday items that transformed their imaginations still bring smiles to our faces, and served as a constant reminder of why we engaged in this project in the first place.

To "Bill Barber" for his endless patience and love, his continued support, frequent runs to the grocery, and willingness to allow us to inhabit the Barber residence for many weekends and a good deal of the summer. A special thanks from Shelli for the inspiration that Nicole and Brent provided. She has been greatly moved by their amazing strength, courage, and their *love* of words.

To the Hogues, for their unconditional love of Sandra; Andre, who keeps her strong; Tarts, who keeps her laughing; and Chuck, who keeps her real. To Paul for his steady and loving support of Laura, and for offering his "spa" setting within which he graciously provided elegant meals to rival any chef. To Mark Condon, Jean Anne's loving soul mate, for his thoughtful opinion, never-ending good humor and wit, his thorough attention and response to our nearly polished draft, and his constant reminder that our work is both groundbreaking and powerful.

For our enduring friendship and one another. We are a fortunate bunch to have come together as we did. Each brings her own unique talents and has shaped our work and this book in important ways. We want to celebrate our laugh-out-loud moments, our moans and hurrahs that have so energized us as we unearthed yet another use for the subtext strategy.

We are grateful to the Center for Collaborative Literacy Development that provided the initial funding that got this project up and running.

For our teacher friends, Angela Hicks and Caryn Walker, for sharing stories of the impact of the strategy on their kids, and Lanita Singleton, who provided enthusiastic response to an early draft of Chapter 2.

To chef and dear friend Mary Wheatley for celebrating us so wonderfully even before this book had seen the light of day. And to other family members and friends who have supported and encouraged us in our journey—we thank you!

Heartfelt thanks to Lois Bridges, our wise and witty editor for her constant and loving support. Her ability to guide us with kind words and gentle nudges was as noteworthy as it was appreciated.

Finally, to the many children whose brilliance is reflected in these pages. Though they are too numerous to mention here, we feel blessed to have shared our lives with them. Their remarkable work and sometimes surprising responses to our efforts to bring literacy to life helped us to grow and learn in ways that cannot be measured.

Introduction

When Shelli Barber, Sandra Hogue, and Laura Wasz were Jean Anne Clyde's students at the University of Louisville, she recognized in each a teacher-researcher in the truest sense, someone whose goals and teaching styles are always open to new ways of supporting young learners. Jean Anne drew this like-minded group together and invited them to join her in a research project, final destination unknown.

Each of us possessed different gifts, and fast friendships were quickly forged. As a research group we really didn't know what we would find, but we were fascinated by the promise of multiple literacies and convinced that we could better support kids as readers and writers by incorporating these literacies into our instruction. Our meetings immediately became a place to share challenges and triumphs and inspire one another as we found our way.

Our method was simple. We brainstormed new ideas and strategies, and Jean Anne coplanned and cotaught with us, our video camera running, as we explored our latest idea. Afterward, we would reflect on what had happened and devise next steps. At our research meetings we shared what worked and what didn't and explored why, eager to understand what was unfolding.

When we came upon the subtext strategy, like bloodhounds, we caught the scent of powerful educational possibilities. We sniffed and followed our noses. As we tracked the strategy through one application after another—reading, crafting and revising, high-stakes testing, and more—we realized we had found a flexible tool that, with a few minor modifications, could be applied in a variety of contexts to help learners of all ages improve their skills as readers, writers, and thinkers. We saw young readers using empathy to connect personally with characters and texts, thus establishing a deeper understanding. Children were identifying and appreciating different perspectives, and, as a result, thinking in more informed ways about the texts they encountered, whether fiction or nonfiction. When applied to the writing process, the subtext strategy helped learners create focused pieces that were full of voice and sensitive to audience needs. To our delight, children used the strategy easily and joyfully! Our data collection and analysis have been ongoing, prompting us to hypothesize about why the strategy feels something akin to magic.

Vygotsky (1978) believed there exists a zone of proximal development, the distance between our "actual development"—the very best we can achieve on our own—and potential development—the very best we can accomplish with help. Interestingly, he also argued, "Play creates a zone of proximal development of the child. In play, a child always behaves beyond his average age, above his daily behavior; in play it is as though he were a head taller than himself" (102).

Although our theory is still tentative, we have come to believe that the success of the subtext strategy is linked to an intriguing mix of empathy, play, and multiple literacies, engaging kids in not just one but a combination of semiotic sign systems. Subtext forms an amazing bridge between thought and written language, capitalizing on literacies with which kids are already deeply familiar.

We invite you to share what we have learned through more than six years of collaboration. Although laid out in sections, our discoveries were not made in the order shared here. And Laura, Sandra, and Shelli have taught different grades over the years, so you'll read about their work with a variety of age levels.

Part I describes our discoveries of the ways in which the subtext strategy can be used as a tool for reading. Chapter 1 introduces our initial explorations with picture and chapter books, while Chapter 2 chronicles our use of the subtext strategy with nonfiction texts as a first step toward helping kids develop a "social imagination" (Johnston 1993) and personalize issues of social justice.

Part II shares ways we have directed the subtext strategy to support all young writers, from English language learners to those considered gifted. Chapter 3 describes how, when combined with kids' own sketches, subtext can breathe emotion and voice into personal writings. Chapter 4 combines the subtext strategy with children's drawings once again, this time as a tool for planning persuasive pieces. And Chapter 5 highlights the ways the strategy can be used to support kids in creating and revising multimedia texts.

Part III describes ways we have used the subtext strategy to prepare our kids for high-stakes testing. Chapter 6 focuses on standardized tests, while Chapter 7 introduces the strategy as a powerful tool for helping kids tackle timed writing-on-demand assessments.

Even as we were writing this book, new uses for the subtext strategy kept revealing themselves. The final chapter, Chapter 8, describes a potpourri of uses for this amazingly versatile strategy, showing how, with simple adaptations, it can be used across the curriculum and with any age group for any number of everyday purposes. Our appendices include important graphic organizers along with lesson plans for Chapters 1 through 7.

We have shared the subtext strategy with numerous audiences, regional and national, since 2001, and the response is always the same: teachers find the strategy, in all its variations, to be simultaneously simple to execute, yet *power filled*. We believe you will, too.

Elliot Eisner (1998) contends that

> becoming literate, in the broad sense, means learning how to access in a meaningful way the forms of life that these meaning systems make possible. What we ought to be developing in our schools is not simply a narrow array of literacy skills limited to a restrictive range of meaning systems, but a spectrum of literacies that will enable students to participate in, enjoy, and find meaning in the major forms through which meaning has been constituted. (12)

We share these practical lessons—lessons we have taught, and lessons we have learned—in the hope that they will enhance your teaching and your appreciation of the remarkable talents all kids carry with them. Ultimately, we hope you will join us in embracing Eisner's "conception of multiple literacies . . . as a vision of what our schools should seek to achieve" (12).

CHAPTER 1

Connecting and Comprehending

The response of engaged readers is intensely visual, empathic, and emotional.

—Jeffrey Wilhelm

In 1999, a group of teachers attending the Kentucky Institute for Arts in Education were visiting the Speed Art Museum. We were standing with J. Daniel Herring, the artistic director of Louisville's Stage One Professional Theatre for Young Audiences, in front of William Edward West's 1849 painting, *The Present* (see Figure 1.1), in which a young woman, surrounded by a group of other people, is examining a necklace she holds in her hands. In the painting, a wide variety of emotions are captured on the characters' faces, emotions we were about to explore firsthand using the concept of *subtext*.

Herring began. "We're going to do an exercise to get you thinking about what the characters in this painting are thinking and feeling. We'll see how that will inform you—the audience—about this painting. We're going to *re-create* the painting, so I'll need some volunteers. Who would like to be the young woman?" Once every character was represented, the volunteers took their positions, duplicating the scene in the painting as a "frozen tableau."

The actors would be bringing the painting to life, but this would

FIGURE 1.1 William Edward West's painting, *The Present*.

involve more than just actions and dialogue. "Actors, try to get inside the characters," Herring continued. "Think about what your character is thinking, what the character is *feeling* in relation to this scene." The volunteers studied the image for clues, mirroring their characters' gestures, thinking about their new identities. "For instance, let's imagine that your best friend buys a new dress and asks what you think of it. You might *say*, 'Oh, how gorgeous!' But you might be *thinking, But it's absolutely* hideous *on* you! So your subtext could be very different from what you would be willing to say aloud. Again, the idea is to think about what your character is *thinking* and *feeling* in relation to others in the painting. Is everyone ready? Focus." The ensemble froze into a three-dimensional version of the painting. "Action!"

The tableau instantly took life. Characters interacted predictably, most oohing and aahing about the exquisite necklace. The "dog" barked convincingly.

"Freeze!" called Herring after thirty seconds, and the three-dimensional image became motionless again. He tapped the shoulder of the person behind and to the bride's far right, who had been smugly fanning herself. She had remained quiet during the scene, conveying her emotions by rolling her eyes and turning her back. Now, sharing her subtext, she revealed a relationship to an absent character, along with bitter emotions. *Oh, it's beautiful!* she snarled. *It's the same necklace he gave me when we were lovers!*

"Action!"

Again the group came to life. The young boy on tiptoe begged to be shown the necklace. "I can't see! May I see it, pllleeease??" When tapped, his feelings about *himself* emerged: *I hate being short! Even Charles is taller, and he's younger than I am!*

"Charles" remained quiet during the lively chatter, interacting primarily with his dog, eyes averted, seemingly deep in thought. When tapped, the actor struggled a bit. "I think he's probably—"

"*Be* the character," Herring encouraged. "Tell us what you're thinking, Charles." The actor hesitated. Then: *Oh please, hurry up. . . . I am so bored! This is girl stuff. I just want to go out and play!*

As the actor portraying the matriarchal older woman interacted with others, she murmured compliments about her daughter's lovely gift. But her subtext revealed a different internal focus. *I'm very impressed with the groom's offering. This young man will be a good husband for my daughter, who deserves the best. This is the perfect gift.*

This continued until each player had shared the character's private thoughts. The exercise complete, we read the placard describing West's painting:

The Present is one of several paintings by West with a bridal theme. In it, the artist depicts a young bride examining a necklace she has been given. The painting is a study of gesture and facial expressions as the bride's family and friends each react to her present. West demonstrates great skill in rendering a wide range of emotions, such as awe, envy, indifference, and joy, on the figures' faces.

The experience had been entertaining, to be sure, but it was much more. The teacher/actors had engaged in *transmediation* (Harste, Short, and Burke 1995; Suhor 1992)—moving the experience from one communication or sign system to another (Solomon 1988), in this case from art to drama. Harste (2000) compares transmediation to

> an instance of metaphor, yet more. Transmediation pushes beyond metaphor by taking what is known in one sign system and recasting it in another. . . . Moving from sign system to sign system is like turning an artifact so that we suddenly see a new facet that was previously hidden from our view. (3)

We had moved from observers of the painting to characters *within* it. Drama had served as a tool, enabling us to step inside the painting to flesh out characters' emotions and personalities. Thus, although the painting was antebellum, we found ourselves making personal connections to the people it represented, whose emotions and issues were not unlike our own.

The implications of this simple drama technique were immediately apparent. Jean Anne remembered the photos of historic paintings in social studies textbooks she had read in school. She and her classmates had never been asked to examine those illustrations and images carefully or to consider what they might learn from them. How much deeper might their appreciation of historical events have been had they been invited to *step inside* those paintings, to walk around inside lives and times that seemed life*less* and incomprehensible?

Soon after this, Jean Anne was rereading Kevin Henkes's *Julius, the Baby of the World* (1995). She had read this book many times before, each time enjoying young Lilly's antics as she came to terms with the arrival of her newborn brother and her role as big sister. Jean Anne had always delighted in the way Henkes integrated dialogue into his illustrations, so they became not mere adornment but part of the story. Each comment added to a more complete understanding of the personalities, relationships, and motives of the characters. Inspired by her experience at the Speed Art Museum, she attended more carefully to the text that Henkes embedded within his illustrations. Sometimes the words were uttered by a single character, other times there were interactions between characters. She wondered, *What would happen if* subtext, *the thoughts* behind *the action, were strategically integrated into the story? How might it impact understanding?*

Drama as a Way of Knowing

Anyone who has seen preschoolers at play knows that they regularly slip into roles of others to "try them on for fit." In fact, so respected is the role of play in early childhood education that play centers are recognized as necessary components of quality preschool classrooms (Bredekamp and Copple 1997).

In their book *Dramatic Literacy* (2001), Lea Smith and J. Daniel Herring argue that "drama can provide a process to learn, by living through or experiencing" (3). Heller (1995) adds, "Drama activities help transform school from a place where we tell students what to think to a place where we help them experience thinking" (13). Similarly, Wilhelm (1997) has documented how integrating drama with reading assisted struggling adolescent readers, impacting their understanding of text as well as their metacognitive awareness while providing real insights into each reader's thinking. Yet despite the fact that drama has been recognized as one way of knowing (Heller 1995; Pappas, Kiefer, and Levstik 1999), it is often an afterthought in schools.

Researchers investigating *perspective-taking* (Emery 1996) have documented young children's struggles to identify with multiple characters in stories (Kegan 1982). Emery observes that "preadolescent readers have a tendency to believe that characters think and feel the way *they* do" (537). To explore this further, she broadened the use of story maps (Baumann and Bergeron 1993), engaging nine-, ten-, and eleven-year-olds in charting characters' perspectives in response to story events. This helped improve kids' ability to infer characters' points of view, leading to a better understanding of both the characters and the story. But what about *younger* children?

Bringing Subtext to the Classroom

In the fall of 1999, the four of us began a collaborative research project in an attempt to unearth the potential of the subtext strategy. Shelli was then teaching second grade at Wheatley Elementary, an urban school serving minority, low-socioeconomic-status students and immigrant children for whom English was a second language. Shelli and Jean Anne chose a story in Shelli's basal anthology so that everyone could examine the illustrations carefully, a vital part of the strategy. *Ruby the Copycat* (Rathman 1991), the story of a "new kid" and her efforts to fit in, was relevant to Shelli's students and would lend itself to exploring subtext.

Before introducing *Ruby*, Shelli and Jean Anne used a transparency of a comic strip featuring both speech and thought bubbles to help kids see what subtext is and how it can be represented. Next, they did a picture walk, using illustrations to make predictions about *Ruby* before reading the story aloud.

"We're going to act out this story a little differently," Jean Anne said, as children immediately began volunteering for roles. "The actors are going to speak for characters, but they're also going to try to imagine what the characters are *thinking and feeling*." She referred back to the comic strip, reviewing how artists distinguish between speech and thought. Then, to help kids understand, she offered the same example J. Daniel Herring had used at the institute. "If Ms. Barber was excited about a new outfit, but I didn't think it looked good on her, I might say something like, 'It's so pretty!' But in my head, I might be thinking, *Ms. Barber, that color looks terrible on you!* I wouldn't say that to her, because I might hurt her feelings. Or maybe seeing her new outfit might get me thinking, *I really need some new clothes!* In other words, subtext is what the characters are thinking and feeling inside their heads."

Not sure whether the kids understood, Shelli and Jean Anne began the enactment, assuring them that eventually they would all have parts to play. Jean Anne was Ruby, Shelli was Ms. Hart, Tracy was Angela, and Kelly was the narrator. "We'll have to read carefully and also look very closely at the illustrations for clues about what each character is thinking." The kids huddled over the text, studying it. Jean Anne told Kelly that she would be interrupting Kelly's reading to invite characters to "tell us what you're thinking."

As the story opens, Ruby is in the doorway, head down, appearing nervous or shy about entering the unfamiliar room. Shelli and Jean Anne invited the kids to brainstorm how the room and the actors should be positioned to match the story's illustrations. Then Jean Anne got into position in the "doorway," like Ruby, and Kelly began reading.

"'Monday was Ruby's first day in Miss Hart's class,'" Kelly read. Jean Anne mirrored Ruby's posture, head down, eyes up. Immediately the kids seemed to take this seriously. Jean Anne held up her hand to indicate she had something to say. *I hate being the new kid*, she interjected. *It's so hard. I miss my friends. What if the kids here don't like me?*

Jean Anne nodded and Kelly continued reading. "'Class, this is Ruby,' announced Miss Hart. 'Ruby, you may use the empty desk behind Angela. Angela is the girl with the pretty red bow in her hair.'"

"Miss Hart, what are you thinking?" Jean Anne asked Shelli, alias Miss Hart.

Shelli looked over Kelly's shoulder, studying the illustration. *Oh, I've got to make sure Ruby feels welcome.*

The narrator continued. " 'Angela smiled at Ruby.' "

"Angela, what are *you* thinking?" Jean Anne asked Tracy, who was playing Angela.

She looks nice.

And so it went. On her way to her seat, Ruby notices the bow in Angela's hair and at lunchtime, hurries home, returning with a bow in *her* hair, launching a pattern of mimicry that typifies Ruby's first week at school. Angela eventually becomes very agitated at Ruby's copying. When Ruby creates a poem that is nearly identical to Angela's, Angela pens an angry note that brings Ruby to tears.

At this point in the story, convinced that the kids understood what to do, Jean Anne and Shelli divided them into "character" groups of three or four. There were multiple Rubys, Angelas and Miss Harts, as well as one group who created subtext for Ruby's unnamed classmates. Each group had sticky notes. "Now it's *your* turn. In your groups, *be* your character. Think like your character. On your sticky notes, jot down what you are thinking and feeling on each page, and put them right in your book." A quick demonstration helped kids see how to do this.

Carlos, Manuel, and another boy were studying a picture of Ruby glancing meekly at Miss Hart, who had kept her after school (see Figure 1.2). "You're Ruby. Look at your face," Jean Anne suggested. "What are you *thinking?*" She wondered whether perhaps this task was incomprehensible for kids who knew so little English.

"I think she thinking. . . ," Carlos began.

"Carlos, *be Ruby!*" Jean Anne encouraged. "Ruby, look at your face. What are you thinking?"

Carlos hesitated for a moment, eyes on the illustration. Then, with a sheepish grin, he said, "I thinking, *Oh, no. I in big trouble!*" Eight-year-old Carlos, a U.S. resident for just six months, was able to participate fully in the experience. Rather than practicing isolated skills on a worksheet, the instruction offered in many ELL programs, the use of subtext had enabled him to delve deeply into the story and access the character's inner thoughts.

Once kids had generated subtext for the remainder of the story, they performed it, one member from each "Ruby," "Angela," "Miss

FIGURE 1.2 Carlos' subtext reveals that he clearly empathizes with Ruby's fears.

Hart," and "kids" group offering their character's thoughts, until each group had shared.

Because *Ruby* had worked so perfectly in Shelli's room, Jean Anne used it again when she introduced the subtext strategy to Laura's second and third graders. She began as she had previously, inviting kids to make predictions about the text based on the cover illustrations and first few pages. She read the book aloud, then demonstrated with Laura and another child how to interject subtext. They rotated actors until they got to the climax of the story: Angela's note to Ruby. Kids then began working in small character groups to create subtext for the remainder of the story.

Carrying the lesson over to another day, Laura and Jean Anne revisited the process, this time using transparencies of the first few pages of the story and writing thought bubbles directly on them. Working together, they created subtext for Miss Hart, demonstrating how they considered *their own* experiences as they imagined what Miss Hart might be thinking:

LAURA: I think Miss Hart might be thinking, *Oh, that girl looks like she's shy. I want to be sure to welcome her.*

JEAN ANNE: And you know what else she might be thinking? *I hope the other kids like her. I hope the other kids accept her right away.*

LAURA: Oh, I can remember when Katy was new; I was thinking, *I hope the kids accept her right away.* [Then, noticing that one student in the illustration is up from her desk] Or she might be thinking, *I wonder why Susie is getting out of her desk?*

[Jean Anne and the class quickly reviewed what happens next in the story: Ruby's "hopping" home for lunch and returning with a bow just like Angela's, the girls exchanging compliments.]

LAURA: Miss Hart has her mouth open, so that might indicate something. From our drawings we know that when people's facial expressions change, they're usually thinking something.

[The kids began offering ideas, too]

TERRESHIA: She's probably thinking, *I can't believe she's coming back to school looking just like Angela.*

JEAN ANNE: Except at this point in the story, I'm not sure that Miss Hart thinks that's so unusual. Maybe she's thinking, *Oh, Ruby's got a bow just like Angela's!*

FALICIA [whose hand was up]: Ooooh—you took mine!

RONALD: Maybe Miss Hart might be thinking, *They look like they're good friends.*

JEAN ANNE: There are a lot of things we could put down, aren't there?!

JESSIE: *I'll bet Ruby's having fun now* [pause] or, *Why are they talking in class?*

The kids seemed to be making good use of the demonstrations, offering sensitive suggestions for the characters' thoughts. Jessie revealed her ability to appreciate the relationship between Ruby and Angela but, like Laura, she was also able to slip into Miss Hart's "discipline" mode, seeing the exchange between the two girls as a potential behavior problem. The kids had begun interpreting characters' motivations based on their own life experiences and the vicarious experiences offered by the text.

When kids returned to their character groups to revisit what they had done and create subtext for the remainder of the story, Jean Anne noticed that Kaitlyn, Jessie, and Tahjah were all writing on individual sticky notes without talking together. The page they were dealing with featured Angela furiously scribbling her note to Ruby. Kaitlyn had written, *I'm going to get her.* Jean Anne asked Jessie what she thought, but she shook her head. "It sounds like she's gonna beat her up." Tahjah, busy working on his own sticky note, didn't hear Jessie's remark. "Kaitlyn thinks Angela is thinking, *I'm going to get her.* What do you think, Tahjah?" "It sounds like she's gonna meet her on the playground and beat her up," he said. On a discarded sticky note, Jean Anne saw that Tahjah had written, *This note will show her to stop copying me.* Apparently the girls hadn't liked that subtext. Jean Anne decided there had been some productive debate among the three before she arrived on the scene.

Jean Anne then joined Shay-wanna and Ronald, who were thinking deeply about their page. She offered to take dictation while they brainstormed. It was obvious that they identified with Angela's anger at Ruby's copycat behavior. As Angela, Shay-wanna offered a very emotional plea: *She's made me angry because she's been copying me all day long!* she began. *I want to tell her, "Can you please,* please *stop copying me?!"* On the next page, Ruby is pictured at her desk crying over Angela's note (see Figure 1.3). Although Angela is not pictured on that page, Shay-wanna and Ronald stayed in character: *I think she will stop copying me for the last time.*

But something else wonderful happened as they more closely examined the illustration of Ruby crying. Ronald, a child who receives special support services, said in a gentle voice, *Maybe I said too bad to her. Maybe I was too mean.* He paused, then added, *Maybe I should tell her I'm sorry.* And even though Shay-wanna understood and clearly felt Angela's anger, she offered a sweet reflection that revealed her genuine concern and a deep understanding for Ruby's perspective as well: "You know, I really like Ruby. She just didn't know how to fit in. She just wanted to play, that's all."

Andrew, Josh, and Marcus, who were channeling Miss Hart, revealed their understanding of her frustration at helping Ruby "be herself." As Ruby reads her poem, remarkably similar to Angela's, Miss Hart's head is down. The boys wrote, *Aw man. Ruby is copying again.* When Miss Hart keeps Ruby after school, the boys offered, *Maybe I should tell her Mom.* Although Angela is not pictured, Terreshia, Elizabeth, and Falicia, imagining themselves in Angela's shoes, were still

FIGURE 1.3 Shay-wanna and Ronald interpret Ruby's gestures. Their ability to empathize leads to deeper understanding.

thinking about Ruby: *I hope she's in trouble.* When Ruby demonstrates her ability to hop (something we've seen throughout the story) and her classmates copy her, another "Miss Hart" group offered, *Oh, at last! Something Ruby's doing on her own! Ruby, you are getting the hang of it. You aren't copying.*

These early sessions using the subtext strategy convinced us that kids were not only capable of making the shift in perspective some had suggested was difficult for them but were able to do so effortlessly. Instead of being bystanders, they had become participants in the story. And the subtext they generated helped us see how deeply they understood the characters and their motives.

Originally, we formed character groups in which two or more kids collaborated, reaching consensus as they generated subtext for a single character. We believed that these conversations were necessary for kids to be able to adopt a new perspective successfully. We still value those rich conversations, but we also have come to see that individual interpretations help everyone get at more dimensions of the characters.

A Strategy That Supports All Readers

Since our initial explorations with the subtext strategy we've all used it with a variety of texts. Sandra introduced it to her six-year-olds the very first week of school as she began an author study of Robert Munsch. She read *Something Good* (1990), the story of a youngster, Tyya, who helps her father grocery-shop, gathering high-calorie junk food in her cart. When Dad commands her to "stand there and DON'T MOVE," the fun begins.

On the next page, we see Tyya with a surprised look on her face. Friends say hello, but she doesn't move. An employee studies her, and knocks on Tyya's head, but still she doesn't move. The following page shows Tyya up on a shelf with a price tag slapped on her nose. "This is the nicest doll I have ever seen. It almost looks real," one shopper observes.

"What do you think she's thinking?!" asked a wide-eyed Sandra dramatically. "Look at Tyya's face!" The kids bunched up close to the book. "Pretend you're Tyya. If someone just put a price tag on *you* and put *you* on a shelf, what would you be thinking inside your head?"

A student said, *Ouch! Stop knocking on my head! I wish they'd just go away, 'cause if I move I'm going to get in trouble.*

"If I were the lady knocking on Tyya's head, I might be thinking, *Is this a statue? Is this a real kid?!*" Sandra added, demonstrating how she stepped inside a character's head. And so it continued, with Sandra reading, pausing periodically to invite kids to provide subtext for characters and offering subtext of her own. Kids were clearly and effortlessly engaged.

Sandra's young students also used subtext to climb inside *Freedom Summer* (Wiles 2001), a story about the U.S. civil rights movement. In this book, two dear friends, one black, one white, are forced to conduct their public lives according to the "whites only" rules of their Southern community. When legislation allows John Henry and Joe to swim together in the public pool, the boys are thrilled and race to town to swim there together for the first time. Jerome Lagarrigue's illustrations feature John Henry's big brother, Will Rogers, and another black worker obeying their boss's orders. The text reads:

County dumb trucks are here. They grind and back up to the empty pool. Workers rake steaming asphalt into the hole where sparkling clean water used to be. One of them is John Henry's big brother, Will Rogers. We start to call to him, "What happened?"

but he sees us first and points back down the road—it means "Git on home!" (n.p.)

"Will Rogers, what are you thinking?" Sandra asked the kids. Several of them stepped into big brother's role, each offering thoughts from Will's perspective:

TI: *What are they doing here? This pool is not going to open. Black people are supposed to come in here but they can't. Just go home.*

BRANDON: *They will not build the pool over again because they're mean. They don't want black people to swim in there.*

RYAN: *I don't want to fill up the pool with asphalt because maybe I wanted to swim in it too. But I have to do what the boss says. I'm mad.*

Next, Sandra asked, "Joe, what are you thinking?"

WHITNEY: *What's going on? There is John Henry's brother and some other workers filling up the pool.*

KAREN: *What are they doing to the pool?*

KARLA: *Why are they doing this?*

"John Henry, how about you?"

JACKY: *What is going on?*

WHITNEY: *I don't know why white people don't think we have feelings, but we do. I'm sad because they're filling up the pool.*

These first graders' subtext provides a glimpse into their understanding of the story, the historical issues the class had been investigating, and the characters themselves. Many of their connections are sophisticated, providing evidence of surprising insights. This is particularly compelling, considering that young children have for years been considered egocentric, unable to appreciate others' feelings or circumstances (Donaldson 1978).

The subtext strategy can also be used with chapter books. Shelli, Laura, and Sandra regularly invite their six- to ten-year-olds to speculate about characters' thoughts during chapter book read-alouds. Despite its informality, offering subtext seems to move kids from the role of passively listening to a text to becoming active participants in the story. We have found it to be a good tool for scaffolding kids who are new to lengthier texts. It's also particularly useful in helping kids comprehend and connect to tender texts (as we like to call them), stories containing difficult or emotionally charged issues. Stepping inside the story helps anchor kids in times, places, and experiences different from their own.

Creating subtext adds amazing depth for high school readers as well. Steven Boros, one of Jean Anne's student teachers, was curious about what his ninth graders would do with the strategy. They had been reading Walter Dean Myers's *Monster* (1999), a chapter book (written as a screenplay) about a teenager on trial for murder. Each day, they had been "performing" the text, a handful of kids reading the various roles. But when they revisited the text adding subtext, the students became very absorbed, exploring subtle aspects of the text that had not been a part of their prior discussions.

The Benefits of Using the Subtext Strategy with Fiction

While the subtext strategy is simple to execute, it has many benefits for readers: it promotes clear, personal connections to the text; it enhances the ability to make inferences; and it promotes a sophisticated understanding of multiple perspectives. Interpretation occurs naturally, made possible by kids' thoughtful "reading" of the illustrations and their insights into the characters' perspectives.

Making Connections

Many researchers identify making connections as a strategy necessary for meaning construction (Fountas and Pinnell 2001; Harvey and Goudvis 2000). Harvey and Goudvis argue:

> When children understand how to connect the texts they read to their lives, they begin to make connections between what they read and the larger world. This nudges them into thinking about bigger, more expansive issues beyond their universe of home, school, and neighborhood. (68)

Generating subtext for characters helps readers step *outside* their own lives, *into* the story, where they seem able to make connections to characters and their worlds. As they become a part of the story, the story becomes real to them.

Making Inferences

"To push beyond the literal text, to make it personal and three-dimensional, to weave it into our own stories—*that* is to infer," argue

Keene and Zimmermann (1997, 152). "When we read, we stretch the limits of the literal text by folding our experience and belief into the literal meanings in the text, creating a new interpretation, an inference . . . the crux of the new meaning" (147–48). For Harvey and Goudvis (2000), inferring is "the bedrock of comprehension" (105), "the play of imagination as we mentally expand text" (153). Creating subtext is a tangible, full-engagement strategy for making inferences about characters and story, helping readers draw conclusions. Essentially, readers tap all relevant resources, combining interpretations of illustrations and text with their own personal experiences to construct a deep understanding. And because their interpretations grow from their life experiences, the subtext they create will be richly varied yet still relevant.

Understanding and Empathizing with Characters

Young children slip easily into drama, stepping into others' shoes as if they were their own. As a result, they develop insights into characters' personalities, intentions, and motives, helping them construct a deep understanding of the text and its characters' varied perspectives. Reading a story becomes a much more complex and complete experience, the characters more realistic, more like the kids themselves. Even the hilarious story of a child who can do no right, *No, David!* (Shannon 1998) becomes more meaningful when we move beyond Mom's scolding words to consider David's motives and feelings as well.

This natural ability to create subtext enables youngsters genuinely to empathize with the characters they "become." Shay-wanna's sweet reflection about Ruby's feelings as she explored Angela's subtext demonstrates this clearly. She was able not only to relate to Angela's anger at Ruby but also simultaneously to empathize with Ruby's emotions. Even Sandra's six-year-olds were able to appreciate multiple perspectives, challenging popular views that young children are unable to de-center, to appreciate others' perspectives.

After using the subtext strategy, most adults have commented on its power to help them think deeply about characters' emotions and motives and appreciate a text from multiple perspectives. When Jean Anne first introduced the subtext strategy to teachers, she used *Ruby,* as she had with kids. Many of these teachers were very irritated with Ruby—until they were invited to step into her shoes and experience the thoughts and feelings of a new kid desperate to be liked. And aside from occasional sarcasm and humor, there is often little difference between adults' subtext and that generated by children. One preservice teacher wrote:

> The first time through the story, I identified with Angela and despised Ruby. After adding subtext and thinking about the entire situation, I began to feel sorry for Ruby. This was an activity we only did once, but it had the biggest impact on my perception of teaching reading.

Linda Christensen (2000), whose work with critical literacy has received recent attention, believes that "to become a community, students must learn to live in someone else's skin, understand the parallels of hurt, struggle, and joy across class and culture lines, and work for change. For that to happen, students need more than an upbeat, supportive teacher; they need a curriculum that encourages them to empathize with others" (2). As Sandra's little ones demonstrated in coping with potentially difficult topics, the subtext strategy naturally supports even very young readers in developing sensitivity to others.

Cecily O'Neill (1990) argues that there is real value in learners "taking on roles": it allows them "to transcend their everyday selves, and get a glimpse of their own potential. . . . But the result is not merely that the participants' role repertoire is expanded. . . . [S]tudents may come to recognize, and . . . modify their habitual orientation to the world" (293). The subtext strategy has enormous potential for helping readers reflect on *their own behavior* and its impact on others. Debriefing sessions where kids share new insights enhance the likelihood that they will modify their interactions with others.

Assessing Comprehension

Finally, kids' subtext provides teachers with a window into the "inner world of the reader" (Wilhelm 1997, 45), allowing us to informally assess kids' comprehension. Whether they are creating and discussing subtext with their peers or weaving imagined subtext into an author's text, children's connections to and interpretations of text are clear and provide evidence of the depth of their understanding of a text and its characters.

Moran (2000) believes that "our reading instruction needs to empower students so they can comprehend real life situations" (38). If kids are invited to examine the lives of others, trying them on for fit, looking around inside the story, feeling the feelings of characters with life experiences different from their own, it's just possible that they might become kinder, more compassionate adults, able to empathize with and appreciate the perspectives of others whose lives at first glance seem incomprehensible or unworthy of consideration. Imagine what a difference that could make.

2

Fostering Critical Literacy

> In the kind of world in which imagination is alive, people have the capacity to look through another's eyes, to take one another's perspective upon the world.
>
> —Maxine Greene

Teachers become enthusiastic when they realize what's possible when kids are invited to look critically at texts with an eye toward issues of social justice. To approach such issues, Barbara Comber (2001) argues that teachers must "help children learn to think about and question texts in ways that develop their analytical capacities and critical reading practices" (2). Christine Leland, Jerry Harste, and Kimberly Huber (2005) agree: "Questions such as 'Whose story is this?' 'Who benefits from the story?' and 'Whose voices are not being heard?' invite readers to interrogate the systems of meaning that operate both consciously and unconsciously in texts, as well as in mainstream culture, to privilege some and marginalize others" (259).

A variation of our original subtext strategy is a useful companion tool to critical literacy practices that examine the construction of messages and the points of view represented. By creating subtext for readers with a vested interest in the issue at hand, kids not only can consider and embrace multiple perspectives, but can do so with rela-

tive ease. In the process, they develop a deep empathy for others that
pushes them to consider all sides of an issue.

Applying the Subtext Strategy to Nonfiction

Unlike fiction texts, which contain characters whose lives we try to
understand and whose faces and gestures—thanks to illustrators—we
can sometimes see, expository texts often contain no people with
whom we can relate. Convinced that the subtext strategy could be
applied to nonfiction materials, we began toying with a variation of
Watson, Burke, and Harste's (1989) planning-to-plan strategy, which
was devised as a tool for creating units of study. They encouraged
teachers to consider their topics from a variety of "discipline" perspectives. "Disciplines" or "knowledge systems"—history, science, ecolo-
gy, for example—"represent various perspectives or ways of structur-
ing knowledge about the world" (Harste 2000, 10). For instance, if
one were planning a unit on farming, thinking like an environmental-
ist would lead to different questions and concerns than thinking like a
farmer or an ornithologist. And each would add richness and authen-
ticity to an inquiry. Though some of the questions and concerns posed
by these "experts" might overlap, others would be unique, showcasing
the value of each perspective.

What if readers were invited to think like a scientist, a geologist,
or a historian as they read a text? How might approaching the piece
from the perspective of a community member—a parent, mayor,
attorney, migrant worker, whomever—impact one's reading of an
informational piece? What if we examined an issue not by simply noting whose voices aren't being heard but by *inviting* those readers' voices to the table?

We decided to select a variety of "texts"—advertisements, commercials, informational texts, political cartoons, editorials, movie
reviews, and so on—and consider them from several different perspectives, creating subtext for imagined readers who would find the texts
relevant. When we shared the results at our next meeting, we realized
we had each approached the task differently.

Jean Anne had begun by asking, "Who are all the different readers of this piece who have a significant point of view?" and sketching
each of them. Her first text was a newspaper article, a lengthy front-
page story detailing the fallout from an area "priest sex scandal." She

FIGURE 2.1 Jean Anne offered subtext for a variety of "readers" of this lingerie catalogue.

first imagined the thoughts of a victim: *How can they let [the Archbishop who concealed the scandal] get away with this? He knew! This could have been stopped. My life has been changed forever.* Then she posited the reactions of two parishioners. One thought, *These priests have behaved so indecently: and we have to pay for their misdeeds.* But Jean Anne thought an older parishioner—like her mom—might think, *Father Joseph's done everything he can. He's a good man.* Her final subtext, for the Archbishop, was, *When will this be over? How can we raise the funds to pay for it? I should've stopped this years ago. Why didn't I?*

Coincidentally, Jean Anne had also looked at a page of a popular women's lingerie catalogue, creating subtext for the husband of a dowdy wife, the mom of young teens, a bride-to-be, and a dietician (see Figure 2.1). She had never considered how many different perspectives there might be about something so ubiquitous!

Shelli had watched a news story about a white girl who, denied admission to Yale, was suing the university for its affirmative action policy. The student objected to black students getting extra points on their applications regardless of family income. Shelli admitted to some bitterness at having been deemed ineligible for certain loan programs herself. "I have sort of been a victim, too, trying to get a teaching job," she told us. After she had created subtext for minority students, she realized that what was happening to African Americans "was not exactly fair either. I began to consider new solutions, where earlier, I was flat against it." She recalled university classes in which students had been asked to defend whatever position was assigned to them. "But I still didn't walk away with a deep understanding of my issue. I don't even remember it; it was more just a surface understanding. Using subtext is more layered than that. I had trouble turning the strategy off!" Jean Anne agreed.

Sandra had chosen a magazine ad for alcohol featuring a photo of a tropical beach. At the bottom in the foreground was a bottle of Crown Royal and the phrase "Paradise Found." Sandra, the daughter of a cigarette factory worker, came to the "reading" with her own set of biases, offended that more attention wasn't being paid to alcohol abuse. She shared her subtext, beginning with an alcoholic: *Yeah, alcohol tastes like that. I get that utopian feeling.* Her potential drinker (teen or adult) thought: *Whoa, I'd like that feeling. Paradise? It comes with the alcohol, so, sure.* Sandra also thought about parents' responses: *I don't want my kids thinking that they can get paradise from a bottle of Crown Royal.*

While Jean Anne, Shelli, and Sandra had been able to shift perspectives for different readers fairly easily, Laura struggled as she tried to apply the subtext strategy to a review of the new *Rugrats* movie. She had deliberately selected an individual with a vastly different cultural background from her own—an African villager—and she was frustrated. "I discovered I didn't have enough information to *be* an African villager," she reflected. That hadn't occurred to Jean Anne, who realized she probably knew enough about each role she chose to enable her to create subtext easily. But the issue was even larger than that. Laura had selected a reader for whom the article was probably irrelevant. An African villager might not have access to the movie and might not be able to read the review. We later realized that kids' *background* knowledge—about the people for whom they were imagining a subtext *and* the concepts and/or topics addressed in a text—would be key to their success with the strategy.

As we continued to think about our experience with applying the subtext strategy in this way, its potential as a tool in support of critical literacy became evident. Stepping inside our readers' worlds had helped us interpret texts in ways we had not originally considered, enabling us to empathize with those readers. This more personal connection softened any hard stances, leaving us more thoughtful about each issue. We couldn't help believing that if kids stopped to think about the perspectives of readers other than themselves, they might become a bit more open-minded, perhaps even fairer to others.

Planning to Introduce the Strategy to Kids

We knew that how we introduced the strategy to our students was important. First, they needed to record their own responses before imagining subtext for other readers. This would enable us to see whether their thinking changed. Second, sketching the imagined readers was essential. "Illustrating pulled me into my readers' personalities," Jean Anne recalled. "It gave me time to enter the reader's world, slowed me down enough to think, *What is this person like?*" Deciding what readers looked like and what they did—their roles or occupations—helped Jean Anne settle into the person she was trying to become. We suspected that sketching would also help kids give life to Shelli's aptly named *invested readers,* those who had some stake in the text's content. Finally, we thought it would be important for at least the older kids to reflect on how creating subtext for their readers had impacted their thinking. This would offer a window into the workings of the strategy.

Taking the Strategy into the Classroom

Our search for texts to use was frustrating. School materials contained little more than facts, not the issues we believed would prompt deeper, multidimensional thinking. So we turned to articles found in our local newspaper. They were challenging, but we tried to choose topics to which kids could relate.

Shelli and Jean Anne tried the strategy in Shelli's room first, using an article about a debate over smoking regulations. They discovered fairly quickly that the article had several tough spots—including the title, which everyone in our research group had to reread numerous times before we understood it: "Tennessee Cities Oppose Law That Prevents Smoking Regulations."

Shelli discussed the title and first paragraph with the kids, then asked them to read the rest of the text independently and write a quick response. As they gathered to talk briefly about their initial impressions, several kids launched into animated and heated diatribes that placed them firmly on one side of the issue or another. They were particularly passionate while debating the effectiveness of non-smoking sections in restaurants:

JARED: It's just a little wall. The smoking still comes over. It's just a little wall.

SHELLI: And sometimes there is not a wall.

SEVERAL KIDS: Yeah!

CLAY: People can die from secondhand smoke.

KRISTINA: That's their choice.

JARED AND CLAY: How's that their choice?!

JARED [*yelling*]: Many people die from secondhand smoke! Eighty thousand a day!

JANISHA: They still have a choice to go into that restaurant.

KRISTINA: I have been in restaurants where the nonsmoking [section] is higher. [*She gestures that the seating was on a higher level.*]

KYLE AND CLAY: It still gets out!

KRISTINA: Well, if that becomes a problem, they should tell the manager.

The room was buzzing with varied opinions, some of which included "interesting" statistics. Clearly, kids from our tobacco-producing state were passionate about this issue!

Creating and Sketching Invested Readers

Next, the kids brainstormed a list of imagined readers who might find the text of interest. The list was lengthy and varied: business people who must eat out often, nonsmokers, children, restaurant owners, bar owners, pregnant women, tobacco farmers, teens (smoking and

FIGURE 2.2 Kids preserved invested readers' thoughts on a sheet like this.

nonsmoking), parents of those teens, drug dealers, the mayor, and the governor. A couple of suggestions—hobo was one—sparked some debate, as kids argued their appropriateness. "Boy, we have a lot of readers," Grace observed as the list was being completed.

"Yes," Jean Anne agreed. "And they may have different opinions of this article, and that is what we want to get at. We're wondering what will happen to *our* opinions of this issue if we step inside different people's shoes."

Shelli asked the students to choose two readers from the list, including one with a viewpoint different from their own. She handed out a subtext thought-bubble sheet (see Figure 2.2 and Appendix A) and asked kids to begin sketching one of their readers in the center.

As Shelli and Jean Anne circulated through the room, they soon realized that the kids were not getting it. Noah had sketched two dead people, complete with XX's over their eyes; another had chosen a young child who wouldn't have had a prayer of reading, let alone comprehending, the text. Others included few details in their sketches, suggesting they would probably struggle with the subtexting strategy. Shelli and Jean Anne instantly recognized the problem. They had failed to demonstrate how to create and sketch invested readers. They quickly gathered the students on the carpet to show them what to do.

At the overhead Shelli demonstrated how she tapped into her experience as a server in a restaurant as she sketched and became Stan, a restaurant owner. She talked as she drew, gradually assuming Stan's persona. "He owns a business, a franchise—maybe a TGI Fridays." She sketched a conservative male face with an abundance of hair, wearing a neatly pressed shirt, tie, slacks, and polished shoes. She then *became* Stan, offering insights about who he was and his world. "I'm Stan. My restaurant serves smokers and nonsmokers. I've been doing this for about six years. I love serving people and making sure they are happy and satisfied when they come out of my restaurant. I am also a nonsmoker who previously smoked."

Next Jean Anne began creating her reader. "My reader is a tobacco farmer. I grew up in farm country, but farmers in New York State grow fruit and vegetables, not tobacco," she said, demonstrating how to bring in prior experience that had relevance as she considered this new reader's point of view. "My reader is a smoker and it's kind of hard for me to step into that role, because I am not a smoker. I really have to think about this person's perspective." Jean Anne named her reader Paul after a farmer she knew, then added the hat she knew farmers wore to protect them from the sun. Then she *became* Paul. "I live a tough life. I am up really early, I rely on what happens with the weather, so I can't count on a steady income." She mentioned the potential for skin cancer due to long days in the sun. "I work on a farm that has been in my family for years. This is our family's business and I am a smoker, though I wish I weren't. I'm just a guy trying to survive. I'm irritated because people are trying to control this crop. My family's been talking about growing other crops, but I don't know if we can really make that happen."

FIGURE 2.3 Eli has reacted to the article as "Spike," a teenage smoker.

As Jean Anne was describing Paul, Eli pulled Shelli aside to show her his sketches of Spike, a teen smoker (see Figure 2.3). When Jean Anne finished, Eli talked about his readers: "I have a teen that smokes and a teen that doesn't smoke. My teen that smokes is one of those guys that always says—you know—'Rad.' He has spikey hair and earrings and stuff."

"Would you like to come up here and sketch him for us?" Jean Anne asked. Eli made his way to the overhead projector and sketched

Spike in detail: a pierced ear, spiky hair, a cigarette hanging from his lips, a speech bubble containing the expression "Rad." He talked as he drew. "Spike likes smoking. All his friends like smoking because they think it is cool. He doesn't want to stop because then his friends won't think he's cool and won't be friends with him anymore. He knows it's bad but still doesn't want to stop. Also it's very hard to stop once you get started. It's a drug and when you don't get to smoke you can have headaches and diarrhea," he added, sounding like a disclaimer from a TV pharmaceutical ad.

"Eli's trying to bring in all he knows about this kind of teenager, and what happens when you stop smoking," Jean Anne observed. This notion of tapping into prior knowledge was something Shelli had been emphasizing in reading.

Eli also jotted down the people who *influenced* Spike. Shelli and Jean Anne had not thought to include that, but they realized it really helped reveal who Spike was. They encouraged kids to think about who influenced *their* readers.

This final think-aloud complete, kids returned to their sketches to revise them and to list their readers' attributes—both personal and professional—on their subtext sheets.

Creating Subtext for the Reader

Next Jean Anne demonstrated creating subtext for her reader. Kids were asked to observe quietly and be prepared to talk about the demonstration afterward.

Jean Anne, in the person of Paul, the tobacco farmer, began reading the smoking regulations article:

> "Tennessee Cities Oppose Law That Prevents Smoking Regulations" *What in the world are they trying to say?* [She records Paul's subtext in a speech bubble.] "1994 Statute Stops Them From Passing Tough Ordinances NASHVILLE, Tenn.—Several Tennessee cities want to repeal a state law that prevents them from regulating smoking in restaurants, bars and other privately owned businesses. At least three bills are pending in the legislature to wipe the 1994 law from the books." *Uh-oh. I am a tobacco farmer and this could be trouble for me. If they regulate smoking, my family farm could be at risk.* "Lexington has enacted a ban on smoking in public places that is on appeal before the Kentucky Supreme Court and has not yet taken affect." *This is big trouble. I need to contact my senator or my legislator.*

At this point, Shelli suggested that Jean Anne be more specific in describing *how* a tobacco farmer might be affected. This was important. Kids needed to understand that they had to be explicit, using the subtext strategy to access all that they knew about the topic. Jean Anne elaborated about Paul's losing money if the ban resulted in fewer buyers for his tobacco, then continued reading:

> "Efforts to regulate tobacco have had a tough time in Tennessee's legislature, where two powerful interest groups—restaurant owners and farmers—tend to oppose them." *They think we have power. I like that. On the other hand I've always hated interest groups and now I'm part of one.*

Next Shelli read the same few paragraphs as Stan, the restaurant owner, again acknowledging how difficult the title was to interpret. As Jean Anne had, she recorded Sam's subtext as she read. "I think my initial response as Stan would be, *I understand this a little bit better than Shelli, because I have been in the business for six or seven years. I know what's been going on politically and have read more about the ban than just this article,*" she told the kids, highlighting how the reader's background experience would impact his reading of a text.

> *They can't do that, ban smoking in public places.* "Meanwhile, Kentucky's General Assembly is considering two proposals on the issue—one to ban governments from regulating smoking and another that would keep cities with smoking bans from receiving money from the national tobacco settlement." *Great. Finally someone understands that the government can't tell us what to do.*

Here, Shelli separated herself from her reader momentarily to remind kids how her experience as a server was helping her imagine Stan's response: "Thinking as Shelli, I remember, when I was a server, hoping that I didn't get the smoking section because I knew I wouldn't make as much money that night. Stan would know that too. As an owner he'd have to think about his servers." Then she became Stan once more.

> *I would be okay with the government telling us what to do if it applied nationally. If they just do it right here in Louisville and not Indiana, guess where my smokers are going to go eat? It's nothing to go over the bridge to eat where you can smoke.*

Shelli went on to show that when Stan considered how the smoking section affected servers' incomes, he began to rethink the issue:

> *I don't think the ban would be a bad idea considering there are lines and lines of nonsmokers, and my servers assigned to smoking don't make as much.*

Once Shelli and Jean Anne felt the kids had a clear sense of how to proceed, they asked them to revisit the article, to generate subtext for the readers they had created. They demonstrated how to bracket and number the text and corresponding thought bubbles to indicate what part of the article the reader was reacting to.

Changing One's Thinking

After they had subtexted for two or more characters, the kids responded in writing to this question: *What happened to your thinking when you created subtext for other readers?*

Initially, Kyle and Kristina had been adamant about their opinions, believing that theirs were the only points of view worth embracing. While creating subtext for invested readers may not have changed their views entirely, they became aware that other people might see things differently. Kyle wrote, "It made me feel like I was actually a different person." Kristina "got the feel of what they thought and felt. So now I give some thought to *their* opinion. Now my opinion is opening up so I can see other things that I hadn't noticed."

Nine-year-old Tyrus, who sometimes struggled with comprehension, adopted something of a storyteller's perspective as he reflected on the experience:

> I found out about how other people feel about the smoking law. I've had some people think, *They can't do this.* Others thought something like, *Whoa, that's great.* But one in particular, Jamie, a boy seven years old, didn't like it. His father, Fred, along with his mother, Susan, also smoked, and somehow the heritage rubbed off on him, and now, citizens of Tennessee, he also smokes. Yep, you heard me right. He, Jamie, also smokes.

Grace, a student whose wardrobe revealed a willingness to be her own person, was completely swept up in the experience:

> I saw the differences and the sames of two or three people. I even caught myself so sucked into my character that was a smoker. She

was against something said in the article and I was her—almost. I found myself yelling at the newspaper. I thought I was against smoking.

My thinking changed in ways I didn't expect at all! All the sudden I'm for smoking, then the next minute I was against it again. Dramatic changes happened. I was a twenty-three-year-old pregnant woman who was against smoking, then I am an eighteen-year-old who smokes. Now I guess, from *my* point of view I say, "It's your choice if you want to smoke or not."

Earlier we mentioned that as we experimented with taking on the roles of various invested readers, some of us found the strategy difficult to "turn off." Nine-year-old Ciarra, for whom thinking deeply about a text was challenging, had a similar response as she became Amy, a mother-to-be:

It was like—I don't want my baby being in restaurants and other places like that because I don't want my baby being around air that has smoke in it, in bars, and why I am writing this, it's like I'm still in her shoes. I can still feel what she thinks and feels—like Amy does not want to go yet, like she wants me to learn more about smoking.

Lessons Learned

It was clear that the subtext strategy was as effective for the kids as it had been for us, pushing them to consider issues from multiple perspectives. And we had learned a great deal from this first attempt to apply the subtext strategy to informational texts. Our most important lesson was how essential demonstrations were to helping kids understand how to create invested readers and how to imagine subtext for them. They needed to see us involved in the process before we could expect them to do it. We all had to lean heavily on prior knowledge, pulling up relevant life experiences of our own to help us enter our readers' worlds. And we were especially pleased that one of the kids had already found a way to enhance the srategy! Eli's idea of considering who *influenced* the reader helped make invested readers three-dimensional.

Second, we had to do better at choosing texts for kids to subtext. We had clearly selected an article that interested kids, but its confusing headline had distracted from the lesson. We would encounter an even greater challenge when working with younger readers.

First and Second Graders Become Invested Readers

While Sandra and Jean Anne believed that Sandra's six- and seven-year-olds could benefit from thinking like invested readers, when they searched for age-appropriate materials that contained some hint of controversy, they found glitz, bells and whistles, or simple—even boring—content that seemed an insult to kids' intelligence. This absence of issue-oriented articles suggests that perhaps publishers assume that young children are incapable of or should be shielded from thinking about sensitive topics.

After paging through countless vacuous publications filled with photos of animal babies, pop culture icons, and games and puzzles that lacked intellectual challenge, Sandra and Jean Anne less than enthusiastically settled on applying the subtext strategy to two advertisements, both found in magazines for kids. One ad, intended for adults, introduced a new minivan; a second was a "kid" ad featuring the *Power Rangers* cartoon show. The plan was to use the adult ad to demonstrate how to create subtext for invested readers, then provide kids with an opportunity to try the subtext strategy for themselves.

"Think about what you know about advertisements," Sandra began, inviting kids to talk with their partners. She and Jean Anne listened as kids discussed and even dramatized commercials they had seen. Zachary, an animated six-year-old, became an actor in a deodorant commercial: "Our deodorant smells goooooood. Other deodorants," he fanned his hand in front of his nose, "ugggh!" Kids laughed and applauded. "Our deodorant," here he rubbed his hand under his arm, "leaves your armpits refreshing clean!"

Nathan defined advertising as "when a company wants you to buy something from them to get more money and they use the money to make more stuff for you to buy." Katlyn agreed, noticing that ads could also be "pictures in a phone book."

"These are persuasive pieces of writing," Sandra told the kids, linking the ads to a familiar writing genre and its purpose. "When companies create an advertisement, they are *intentional* in what they want you to think about. They spend lots of money and lots of time trying to come up with the perfect ad to persuade you—the *reader*—to think in a certain way."

Next, Jean Anne reviewed the subtext strategy. "Today we're

going to try to think about what people who are *looking at* an ad might be thinking in their heads." She held up the minivan ad while Sandra read the print to the kids, then focused on its intended audience. "Do you think this is an advertisement for kids or moms and dads?"

"Moms and dads!" the kids said in unison. Jean Anne then explained that she and Sandra would first offer subtext as themselves, sharing "what we're thinking and feeling inside our heads." Later, they would show how to create subtext for other readers. After the kids had watched the demonstrations, they would do the same with an ad intended for children.

Sandra read the ad: "We are about to take the minivan in a whole new direction." Then she showed how she made personal connections to this "text," pausing to indicate what parts of the ad prompted certain thinking:

> This makes me remember when I had a minivan. People with a van have kids and stuff. I don't have kids, but that was my favorite vehicle. And it kind of makes me miss my van. Under the photo, it talks about new things like sensors that make a sound when you're about to back into stuff. I was thinking, *That would be kind of cool.* In the photo I see those folding down rolling seats, and I think, *My sister is in a wheelchair. Maybe, if I took that seat out, there would be some way to get her in there. I would love that.* But my minivan was the most expensive car I ever had, which is why I don't have one now. *I wonder if adding all those features will make it more expensive than the one I had?*

Jean Anne then demonstrated how she would approach the ad:

> They want to attract my attention with these pictures, and, of course, it is the first thing I look at. And if I like it enough I might read the print, too. *Gosh that looks like the station wagon we used to drive when I was a little kid, except it's got a lot more room. The large luggage compartment would've been great when we went to California when I was a little girl. Look at these seats! We had a station wagon with three seats, and the third seat faced backwards, and it was really fun riding in it. I'm getting good feelings as I read this.*

Jean Anne continued sharing her thoughts, noting how much more spacious the van seemed to be, a definite plus for her family of eight when she was growing up. Then she shifted her thoughts to a concern she has as an adult: "There is another part of me that's thinking, *You know these are gas guzzling cars. They put out a lot of pollution.* That's making me wonder, *What about its air quality standards?"*

Sandra offered more of her subtext. *"And what about these movable seats, which can be 'reconfigured with one hand'? How easy is one seat to remove? They say 'easy,' 'with one hand,' but I don't know about all that. If it's that easy to remove, it will also be that easy to come loose accidentally."*

"I also think that a seat that comes out might be hard to put back," Joseph added.

Next Jean Anne invited kids to consider how an advertiser might change the ad to appeal to a kid audience. A TV was a must, but in the back, because, as Autumn noted, "If it is in the front the person in the front might want to watch it while they're driving." Kids also suggested video games, convertible tops, and sports equipment.

Finally, Sandra and Jean Anne assumed the thinking of other potential readers, just as Shelli and Jean Anne had done with the smoking ban article. Sandra created subtext for someone traumatized by an accident with a large van, Jean Anne for a person who felt her life had been saved because she had been driving a van.

Jean Anne displayed an overhead transparency of an ad for the *Power Rangers* television show, then gave each child a copy to examine. The kids were asked to sketch themselves in the middle of a subtext bubble sheet and record their subtext in response to the ad (Figure 2.4 is Joseph's filled-in sheet). Here's what some other students "thought" as they examined the ad as themselves:

KIMBERLY: This is for boys. My brother would like it. I'm glad they tell what time it comes on.

CORISSA: Why are they trying to get us to watch it? Why would they put it on mornings at 8:30?

CHARLES [*after some initial hesitation because he "knows mom won't like it"*]: It makes me want to be a Power Ranger.

KAIRA: I see swords. This doesn't look like a good show.

Jean Anne and Sandra then invited kids to shift perspectives, as they had done with the minivan ad, this time drawing their moms (or grandmas, aunts, etc.) and dads (grandpas, uncles, etc.). Jean Anne asked them to think first like the woman they had sketched. "Let her voice come out of your head."

"Shift that perspective," Sandra added. "What does *she* think when she looks at the ad?"

FIGURE 2.4a Jospeh first captures his own thoughts about the *Power Rangers* ad, then generates subtext for Mom and Dad (see Fig. 2.4b).

When viewed through the kids' eyes, their female family members had a good deal in common:

JOSEPH'S MOM: It looks too violent. I don't like it.
KAIRA'S MOM: I don't think this will be good for Kaira. I don't think that is good for Kaira because they are fighting with swords. Kaira may get scared.

FIGURE 2.4b (continued)

DAYTON'S MOM: I think it is too violent.

CORISSA'S MOM: Why would our children want to wake up at
    7:30/8:30? Swords? Why would they want to watch this? I hate
    this show because they have swords.

KATLYN'S MOM: I don't like *Power Rangers* because it has fighting and
    I don't like fighting.

SHAKIERA'S MOM: That's for little boys because they watch that all
    the time.

Charles's subtext for his mom was particularly interesting, indicating his awareness of her desire to understand *his* point of view: *"Why do they have swords, costumes? Why does he love these cartoons?"* This "double" perspective is remarkable for a seven-year-old; he recognizes that his mother genuinely does not understand his passion for these pop culture icons.

When the kids subtexted for male family members, sometimes the men agreed with the women's perspectives and sometimes they didn't:

CORRISSA'S DAD: I don't like it because my kids don't watch those kinds of cartoons. I don't know about this. I don't think Corrissa would want to watch this.

CHASE'S DAD: I like it because it has swords.

While imagining his dad's subtext, Aaron wondered about the gender of the Power Rangers: "Why is there one girl Power Ranger?" This led to a debate about the gender of the show's masked characters. Jean Anne and Sandra, who had never seen the show, were of little help. But we later wondered about the meaning behind Aaron's subtext: was he seeking equity in the show or condemning women who fight? In any case, the subtext strategy allowed substantive issues worthy of further discussion to emerge. The shifts in perspective made possible by the strategy create new thinking and questioning, even for six- and seven-year-olds.

The Benefits of Creating Subtext for Invested Readers

Living through the process with kids solidified the benefits of creating subtexts for invested readers. We are surprised at the breadth of these benefits, but no doubt there are others as yet unrealized:

- It pushes us to *respond* to an author's message from a variety of perspectives. This responding is made possible by drawing on prior knowledge, and therefore results in a deeper comprehension of that message.

- It enables us to sidestep the intentions of the author—whether noble or manipulative—and imagine the responses of others with a vested interest in the piece. In many ways, what we experienced mirrors the impact that writing monologues had on Bill Bigelow's high school students

(Christensen 2000). "We feel, rather than observe from a distance. . . . [T]he very act of considering 'How might this person experience this situation?' develops an important 'habit of mind' " (135).

- Points that at first seem minor become amplified when viewed as a reader whose perspective is unlike our own. When reading as ourselves, we tend to pay attention to information that pertains to our lives, at times overlooking parts of a text that don't resonate with us. But when we create subtext as invested readers, we seem to notice more, to read more deeply, and this new information can help us see the world differently.

- It brings us face to face with our own insufficient knowledge base, propelling us to become more informed about the issue at hand.

- It helps us develop the "social imagination" (Johnston 1993) that enables us to appreciate others' lives, values, and concerns. Developing empathy for those whose positions are different from our own encourages us to be less judgmental. Even if we don't agree with another point of view, we seem able to appreciate that perspective, that "truth."

- It helps us become more aware of potential readers' responses to our own writing (see Chapter 4)—better able to anticipate readers' needs.

- Issues once seen as having black-and-white positions move to having shades of gray, to having consequences that impact the lives of others.

- Applied to the reading of advertisements, it helps learners get in touch with the ways in which advertisers attempt to manipulate them and forces them to question the motives of the storyteller. They become more informed consumers who are able to weed out substance from gimmicks.

A final story, told by Angela Hicks, a fifth-grade teacher who recently explored the subtext strategy with her kids, helps make the point of how the strategy relates to social justice:

> During a recent literacy course I took with Jean Anne, I found myself doing a lot of reading and having heated discussions that, for me, held the issue of social justice at their foundations. While I found this topic important, I had not the first notion how to bring this idea to my fifth graders in a meaningful and purposeful way. Teaching in a predominantly white, middle-class school, where during this particular year I had no students of color and only two children who qualified for free/reduced-price lunch, I

was left wondering how I could possibly help my students take a step toward working for social justice within the confines of our learning community. The subtext strategy proved to be a powerful road to follow on our journey.

Throughout the year, we broached topics that the Supreme Court wouldn't touch—the right to die, the placement of the Ten Commandments in public buildings, the Iraq War, child labor, and steroid use in baseball. In fact, by the last few months of school, kids were bringing in newspaper articles, asking for the opportunity to create subtext for them.

One morning while scanning the newspaper before the first bell, a couple of students found an article about and photograph of a man who weighed over seven hundred pounds. The kids were spellbound and rushed to me, requesting that they be allowed to subtext the article. While we had already used the strategy for several newspaper and magazine articles, none of the subjects had ever dealt with people similar to our community members. But this one came a little too close to home, since several students were struggling with their weight.

I knew that the kids were probably more interested in the down-and-dirty details of the article than any issues of justice that might be revealed, so I discouraged the idea, telling them that I wasn't sure we'd have time, secretly hoping that it wouldn't be so intriguing the next day. They took my answer in stride, but by midmorning, the article had circulated throughout the classroom, so everyone knew how many hamburgers the man ate at one sitting, that he needed help with personal hygiene, that he hadn't been able to leave his home in years, and that (to their amazement) he had a girlfriend. Somewhere in the middle of all of this, Michael, a well-liked but overweight eleven-year-old boy, approached me: "Mrs. Hicks, we need to subtext."

Michael's parents had met with me earlier in the year, concerned that he might be showing signs of depression. They had separated soon after school had started and since then he was having trouble sleeping, showing no interest in friends, extremely quick to tears. They acknowledged his weight problem and felt that this, coupled with their separation, was causing school to become painful for him.

Since the conference, I had paid particular attention to

Michael. He was slow to take initiative in any activity, even on the playground. However, he was always included, even sought out for his even-handedness and sense of fairness. The kids respected his gentleness and were sympathetic to his parents' impending divorce. But he was extremely critical of himself, crying over the most insignificant mistake. I was hesitant, but honored his request.

The kids were quick to list people who would be interested in this article—invested readers—most of them choosing someone who could fix this man, like a doctor offering free treatments or a fitness trainer setting up an exercise program. Others were insurance companies saying they shouldn't have to pay for healthcare for someone with no self-control. Michael complained that no one was representing fat people, so a couple of brave individuals (I among them) took on that task.

As I put myself in the skin of an obese man, I discovered some of my own prejudices. I really thought he wasn't trying, that he just needed a little self-control. The subtext I created was the first time I truly realized his pain, his frustration, his fears, and his dreams. I couldn't help but wonder if the overweight kids in my classroom had felt the impact of my own negative views.

As the kids shared, the room became quiet. I think we were all feeling pretty guilty by the time we finished. Finally, Michael said, "I just wanted you to know how I feel. I just wanted you to know."

Did we rid the world forever of injustices suffered by the obese? Did we even rid our classroom of bad jokes and teasing? Probably not. However, one student did find a very effective way for his peers and his teacher to experience a small portion of his life, if only in some speech bubbles on a paper.

★ ★ ★

Dozier, Johnston, and Rogers (2006) argue:

Children and their teachers must both see what they can do with literacy and what it can do for them. . . . Critical literacy involves understanding the ways in which language and literacy are used to accomplish social ends. Becoming critically literate means developing a sense that literacy is for taking social actions, an awareness of how people use literacy for their own ends, and a sense of agency with respect to one's own literacy. (16, 18)

For us, what's most remarkable about this story is the way in which Michael used the subtext strategy to leverage literacy on his own behalf. This child, who related so well to the pain experienced by the obese man, knew that in creating subtext for this man, his classmates would empathize with both the man and with him. Though highly regarded by his friends, he insisted that his friends engage in the strategy, knowing that ultimately it would help them better *understand* him.

Whether used to step inside issue-rich stories or to view an event or idea as an invested reader, sketching and creating subtext for invested readers engages kids emotionally and intellectually. Later, in Chapter 4, you'll see how the strategy can be shifted yet again, this time to support kids in crafting thoughtful written arguments in order to take social action.

CHAPTER 3

Developing Narrative

Images at any age are part of the serious business of making meaning—partners with words for communicating inner designs.

—Ruth Hubbard

Soon after we discovered that children could step inside a story, interpreting illustrations—characters' facial expressions and gestures—along with text to predict the characters' thoughts, we began inviting them to illustrate their own work, to use two forms of literacy to make and share meaning. Like others (Gallas 1994; Harste, Woodward, and Burke 1984; Hubbard 1989, 1996; Martens 1996; Rowe 1994), we observed that the opportunity to incorporate a *sign system*—drawing—with which they were already so familiar was comfortable for kids. Drawing, representing ideas with pictures, is essentially a form of thinking (Ernst 1994) that gives kids a fresh perspective, pushing them to reexamine their work and then supporting them as they translate thoughts into writing for revision. We were groping our way toward using the subtext strategy as a tool for writing.

Sketching to Focus, Sketching to Revise

In the spring of 2000, doll maker Martha Thomas did a puppet-making workshop with Laura's second and third graders. Watching kids talk to, for, and with their puppets—a natural form of play—Laura realized that the puppets had become characters. The kids went far beyond the basic patterns Martha had provided and designed clothes, homes, and personal vehicles for their characters. In essence, they were creating short stories about them. Like Rowe (2003), who used puppets with first graders, Laura found that the immediacy of the puppets and the scenes the kids had created for them helped them understand the concepts of character and setting more easily. Their characters' "problems" emerged effortlessly.

However, although the kids had naturally and eagerly assumed the roles of actors, directors, and oral storytellers, when they put their work on paper, their short stories were long and convoluted, going round and round with no focal point. Jennifer, a fairly fluent writer, wrote a rambling four-page piece about a space alien getting into trouble while visiting earth. Vincent was an avid artist who had learning difficulties that caused him to see himself as a nonreader/writer. At home he would get his sister to write for him. At school he would dictate to his friend Keith, making it difficult to tell what part of the story was really Vincent's. Vincent's first draft of his short story was obviously Keith-written, a lengthy, directionless piece about a disc jockey/rapper.

Laura recognized that when children hold an idea in their minds, the images can be changeable and fleeting; but when the idea is transferred from the imagination and preserved on paper in a sketch, however rough, it is made real, tangible. It is held still and can be closely examined by the writer. So to help her students find a focus, Laura turned to visual art.

She invited her students to sketch the most important part in their pieces. Jennifer's drawing of her alien in front of a grocery store, unable to make herself understood or to read the signs, helped her see that the point of her story "Green Has a Problem" was communication. Her solution? Speech lessons for the alien.

When Vincent drew the most important scene of his piece and began telling Laura about it, his real story—not Keith's—came out. Vincent's drawing (see Figure 3.1) shows a rapper who has lost his voice just before the big show, speechless, peering around the curtain as the crowd shouts his name. Perhaps Vincent's own feelings of frustration are evident in how large the sound-system speaker is and how small and helpless the voiceless DJ is.

FIGURE 3.1 Vincent's sketch perfectly captures the "problem" in his story.

Creating visual representations gave kids a direction for revising their drafts, helping them see the main idea and think about where their stories were going. All their problems weren't remedied by these sketches, but they had created a concrete reference point. Using drawing as a tool for revision enabled the kids to continue to work on their pieces much more calmly and effectively.

Stepping Inside Sketches to Articulate Emotion

Shelli's second graders had been drafting personal narratives, pieces required for their writing portfolios, but they were unable to move forward. The writers had been very reluctant to reread their drafts to see if they made sense for their readers. They seemed consistently able to use drama to identify gestures and emotion that *belonged* in their pieces, yet they seemed unable to convey those details in writing. When Shelli and Jean Anne heard about how Laura's invitation to sketch the most important scene had helped her kids focus their pieces, they wondered if sketching could help Shelli's kids revise their pieces, too.

Jean Anne joined Shelli in the classroom. They began by revisiting George Ella Lyon's *One Lucky Girl* (2000), the story of a family whose trailer was struck by a tornado. They asked the kids to identify the most important scene in the story. After some debate the kids chose the page that pictured the family's discovery that their infant was missing. Next Shelli and Jean Anne asked the kids to study the illustrations and imagine subtext for family members. They also invited kids to talk about how the illustrator had conveyed these powerful feelings and to include these kinds of gestures as they sketched the most important scene in their own drafts.

With their own sketches complete, kids came to the author's chair one by one to present their most important scenes, displaying their sketches as they told the stories captured in their personal narratives. Brandon held up his sketch of himself riding a roller coaster for the very first time, heading down the first big hill. He referred to his illustration as he explained how the event unfolded, entertaining his classmates with a dramatic scream: "I said, 'AAAHHH!!! AAAAAHHH!!' " As Brandon told about his wild ride, Shelli and Jean Anne asked him periodically whether the details he was providing were in his draft. They weren't. Brandon, like the others who had shared, had represented an emotion in his sketch, and it was precisely parts like that—"where you feel something," Jean Anne told them—that kids had to find ways to convey to readers *in writing*.

"I didn't tell them because . . . ," Brandon began. Then, reliving the moment, he tucked his chin, crossing his arms over his chest. "I was going to put my head down like this, but I wanted to hold on to the thing they put in front of you." He stretched his arms out in front of him, squeezing the air as if it were the bar that keeps riders safely in their seats.

"But what were you thinking?" Shelli asked. "As a reader, I want to know what is in your head."

Again, Brandon used gestures to convey his story, jerking his body from the left, to the middle, to the right, as he explained how the "turns were so fast." He seemed so clear about what it was he wanted to communicate. Yet thus far, he had been unable to commit those thoughts to writing.

"Brandon, you will have readers who have never been on a roller coaster," Jean Anne explained. "You'll have to describe it."

"I did tell that my heart was going to jump out of my chest," he said.

"Yes, you did," Shelli acknowledged. "So tell us what you were thinking when experiencing the roller coaster ride."

As Brandon talked, Shelli and Jean Anne jotted his new ideas on sticky notes. "I was just squeezing so hard," he said, continuing his dramatic reenactment. Again his hands squeezed the imaginary bar, his face contorting to convey the fear he felt. "I was actually all balled up."

"What were you thinking, Brandon?" Shelli asked again.

" 'I'm gonna fall outta this thing!' " Shelli quickly jotted his emotion-filled line on a sticky note, then exchanged a glance with Jean Anne. At that moment they recognized the potential of the subtext strategy as a revision tool for young writers.

What were you thinking? Shelli and Jean Anne began to ask that question every time kids shared drawings, capturing on sticky notes the words kids used to convey the feelings present in their illustrations. Using the gestures in their sketches as a support language, the kids now seemed able to step inside their own work, as they had so easily done with picture books. Once inside, they were able to record their thoughts and emotions on sticky notes. They were moving closer to that previously elusive connection between drama and print.

Combining Sketches and Subtext to Breathe Emotion into Kids' Writing

After hearing about Shelli's experience, Laura tried combining the subtext strategy with sketching to support her second and third graders as writers. Adapting a district handout, she asked the children first to draw the most important part of their stories in the middle and then write a brief rough draft of what happened before and after in the spaces above and below the drawing. The children set to work; as usual Laura wrote alongside them.

Samantha started to draw one story, about receiving an award, but then said, "That's not the story I want to tell. Can I tell a different story?" "Just use the back of your outline," Laura told her. But rather than draw and write, Samantha only drew (see Figure 3.2). The next day, Laura had the children write first drafts. Based on her drawing, Samantha wrote:

> One day I was at my mama's house sitting on the soft brown carpet
> watching TV. Then my mom rushed into the house. She said,
> "Samantha your dad has been hurt." I went to the hospital to see

FIGURE 3.2 Samantha first preserved her story using sketches. Note that in her first image, even her mother's sharing the news about the accident is conveyed with a picture.

my dad. He was doing fine. Then the day before the other day, he came home and we took care of him.

Then Laura told the children, "Now I want you to tell your whole story just in drawings." Samantha knew her story well and swiftly drew her pictures, confidently numbering them.

Next Laura asked the children to create subtext for the characters in their drawings. The children were quite familiar with subtext as a

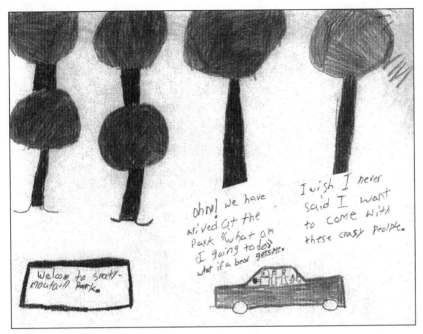

In the drawing: "Welcom to smorky-moutain Park.", "oh no! we have arived at the Park !! what am I going to do? what if a bear gets me.", "I wish I never said I want to come with these crasy peolpe."

FIGURE 3.3 When Joshua subtexts his sketch of a family outing, we sense his fear of encountering a bear. In actual fact, they did!

reading strategy, so they easily applied the process to their own illustrations (Joshua's work is shown in Figure 3.3).

Thinking aloud, Laura then demonstrated how to lift the subtext from her own drawing and determine how and where to integrate it within her written draft. Kids then returned to their seats to incorporate subtext into their pieces. In Samantha's final draft, even her lead is a reflection of her subtext.

I Hate That Building!

by Samantha

I thought my dad was going to die.

One day I was at my mamaaw's house sitting on the real soft brown furry carpet watching television. I hear the door knob go round and round. My mother was trying to open the door. I was thinking, "I wish I could stay a little longer. I am having fun watching TV. I don't want to miss my favorite show."

Then my mom rushed into the house. She cried, "Samantha your dad has been hurt." I got very sad. I almost cried. My mom said, "A piece of the building that he was working on fell on him and knocked him off the ladder and then the piece of building landed on his chest and broke his ribs."

I got real seriously mad at that building. I wanted to smack that building so hard that the building would be in pieces.

We drove to the hospital. I was thinking, "I hope my dad doesn't die. I want my dad to live. I just hate that building."

The hospital was filled with white. The bed was soft and the pillow was fluffy.

Right next to my dad was a very nice man. He talked to my sister but my sister didn't answer him. She said she did not hear him.

My dad had on one sock. His shirt collar was blue. I don't know why my dad had on one sock. My dad's shirt was too long for him. I was way too worried. "I want my Dad to come home right now," I said to myself in my head.

The doctor said, "If the piece of building went two inches closer he would have died."

I left the hospital in a jiffy the first time. I was thinking, "I hope my dad is going to be fine."

He stayed four days. I went to see him. On the way I thought, "I can't wait to see my dad. He is so nice."

I was sitting on the black soft couch watching TV again. I was waiting for my dad to come home. I was sad. I was thinking, "When will Dad come home? I can't wait."

I was glad when my dad came home. I hugged his warm chest where his scar is.

He still has that scar. It's a very small scar.

I took more care of him than all the rest. I really do love my dad. If he dies, I'll be crying a river.

If we compare Samantha's finished piece with her early draft, it's easy to see the impact of the subtext strategy. By stepping inside her own memories, Samantha had to consider *her own* feelings more deeply. She used the insights gained to enliven her piece with emotion and voice.

First Graders Try Sketching and Subtexting

Sandra's six-year-olds were working on personal narratives, too. Typical of young, less experienced writers, her kids often wrote "bed to bed" stories (Graves 1994), describing an entire day from sunup to sundown. Sandra was convinced that even young kids had more compelling stories to tell than the ubiquitous tales of trips to the local amusement park. She wanted her young writers to share more memorable pieces, events they would remember forever. She finally found a theme that seemed right: I Wish It Never Happened stories.

Sandra's students often sketched and wrote in their writers' notebooks about things they cared about, anchoring them in the context of their daily lives. However, they almost always included insignificant details that diluted the essence of the event. Sandra needed a way to keep her young authors focused on only the relevant details of their stories.

Sparked by Laura's idea to sketch the most important scene, Sandra came up with a more detailed version, a three-scene storyboard. Using newsprint folded into thirds, kids would first sketch in the center box the most important scene of their stories—the uh-oh moment, as Sandra called it—the event they wished had never happened. Then, in the first box kids would sketch the scene or event *just before* the uh-oh moment. In the third box, they would sketch what happened *just after* the big moment.

Sandra introduced the idea through a process demonstration (Smith 1983), sketching the uh-oh moment of her story, something that happened when she was four. Sandra and her siblings used to sneak into the chest freezer and scrape ice from the freezer wall, combining it with Kool-Aid to create homemade "poor folk" snow cones. "While everyone else was watching TV, I went for some ice and noticed Mom's hammer in the freezer. I decided to find out what the hammer tasted like, so I lifted it out of the freezer, put it to my tongue and had a lick. But, *uh-oh*!" Kids' eyes bulged, mirroring Sandra's horrified expression. "The hammer stuck to my tongue! Guess what I tried to do?" As Sandra shared what happened, she quickly began sketching the uh-oh moment in the middle of her three-panel page (see Figure 3.4). "The most important part I have right here in the middle, because that's the part I didn't want to have happen." Next, she sketched the first scene—what happened just before that memorable moment, slyly peering into the freezer. Finally, she sketched the outcome—her mom pouring warm water on tearful Sandra's tongue.

Then the kids told their own stories within their response groups; listeners had lots of questions! This oral rehearsal prepared kids to tell a more complete story. Next, they sketched the I Wish It Never

FIGURE 3.4 Sandra's images show that simple sketches are all it takes for an adequate demonstration. But the demonstration itself is essential!

Happened events, following the format Sandra had demonstrated: first the most important scene—the uh-oh moment—then the scene *just before,* and finally what happened *just after.* (See Appendix B for Trifold Template.)

After this, the kids returned to their response groups and used their drawings to tell the story yet again. Some were beginning to see that each time they told the story they got better at it. Finally, they generated drafts of their narratives, using the events in their drawings to tell the story. The oral and visual rehearsals had helped them focus their pieces.

Sandra then demonstrated the next step in the process: how to generate subtext for one another's narratives. First, she explained in detail what was happening in each of her pictures. As she told about her drawings, her "readers"—Jimmy and Jean Anne—asked questions for clarification. Her sketches provided support as she read her draft. Once they understood each scene, Jimmy and Jean Anne offered subtext for the people in Sandra's piece, imagining what they might have been thinking.

For the first sketch, of Sandra sneaking up to the freezer, Jean Anne offered, *I love this stuff, but I'd better be quiet.* Jimmy added, *I better be quiet. Momma will kill me if she catches me.* Viewing Sandra's uh-oh moment, Jean Anne suggested, *I wonder what this tastes like. If it's frozen, it must be good.* But Josh went right to the trauma, offering, *I hope I don't pull my tongue out!*

Similar things then took place in the response groups. Peers supported one another by offering subtext for each other's sketches and drafts. Some kids even discovered that the subtext suggested by group members was not aligned with the feeling they wanted to convey in the piece. For instance, Krystal was writing about a fight with her older brother. The subtext suggestions from her response group were off-base; but they prompted her to recall details of the event. In the end, she was able to offer subtext that more accurately reflected her own feelings.

Joseph had great potential as a writer, usually creating stories that were genuinely interesting. But he had not yet established the level of reader awareness needed to produce a solid piece. The trifold sketches helped him capture and preserve the essence of his story. Here's his draft:

> One Halloween morning my mother woke me up and told me to take out the trash and I cut my foot on a beer bottle and it hurt and hurt. And my mother took me in the house and called the doctor. She got me there right away. We finally got there. The doctor said I had infection. It hurt. He put my foot in a hot thing of water. It really hurt. It stung and stung for a long time. It even burned a long time.

Adding subtext breathed life into Joseph's subsequent draft; its emotion and voice make it much more memorable for readers:

Because My Mom Asked Me

My mom busted into my room. I was still in bed. My mom woke me up. She told me to take out the trash. I thought, *Bummer, couldn't she make Dusty do this?*

I cut my foot on a beer bottle. *Ow! I wonder what on earth I stepped on?* It was like a nail hammered into my foot. I screamed and my mom ran outside. My mom took me inside. Mom cleaned my foot. Then she put four band-aids on it. Mom called the doctor the next day because my foot kept bleeding. It hurt real bad. She got me there right away.

In the doctor's office I thought, *She could make my*

brother do it! Oh, this really really hurts. Oh, why didn't she make my sister take it out? The doctor put my foot in a hot thing of water. It burned and kicked and pounded like a hot tub. He bandaged my foot.

Now I wear my shoes when I go outside.

The trifold sketches enabled Sandra's young writers to create pieces that were sequential, meaningful, and absent of irrelevant details, qualities that demonstrate a real awareness of audience. The sketches were also a tool for capturing details about characters and setting.

Differentiating Naturally to Support Both Struggling and Gifted Writers

Much attention is being paid to "differentiating instruction" (Tomlinson and Eidson 2003; Yatvin 2004) to meet the needs of all learners. We've discovered that the subtext strategy, which combines children's own drawings with their seemingly innate ability to enter others' worlds, naturally supports both the struggling *and* the gifted writer!

As you read the following piece, penned by eight-year-old Chloe, study the level of detail in her illustration (see Figure 3.5), one of many in her book. As she worked, Chloe moved back and forth between sketching and drafting many times, using both to craft her story. But the piece gained even more life once the subtext strategy was added to the mix. Her subtext—originally jotted on sticky notes that she attached to her sketches—can be easily spotted. Consider how integrating her inner thoughts impacts the quality—the *emotion and voice*—of her piece.

Very Bad Tae Kwon Do
by Chloe

As I set my foot inside Tae Kwon Do class, I saw the other students zooming around the room, some even faster than me.

"What if everyone laughs at my glasses?" I asked my mom. I hugged her tightly. I didn't want to go out there.

"It'll be okay, sweetie," she said.

There were some soft colored fabric blocks and balls scattered around the floor. I was very nervous when I looked around. After I undid my sneakers and stepped onto the

"This is gonna be bad," I said to myself. And it was. The music coming out of the stereo in the corner was <u>SO LOUD</u> that it was like 9,000 blasts of thunder going down all at once. We all had to do <u>EVERY</u> command <u>perfect.</u> This definetly was <u>not</u> good.

FIGURE 3.5 Chloe's drawing perfectly portrays her own gestures, which so clearly convey the emotions she experienced. Her visuals extend the meanings expressed in her text. Combining drawing and subtext enables readers to empathize with Chloe.

rough, gray carpet, socks still on, I ran as fast as a bolt of lightning going around 5,000 miles per hour. A few minutes later, an instructor showed up.

"This is gonna be bad," I said to myself. And it was. The music coming out of the stereo in the corner was SO LOUD that it was like 9,000 blasts of thunder going down all at once. We all had to do EVERY command *perfect*. This definetly (sic) was *not* good.

Every time I did something wrong, I put my hand to my chest. I practically felt like I was going to throw up.

"I don't feel so good," I said to myself. And there was NO WAY I could get out of this place.

To respond to the instructor, we always had to say,

"YES SIR!" We got to do sort of the same thing as the adults were doing later (they had classes for them too). This was the idea: You had to start at one block, run to one pad, punch it, go around another block and do the same things except KICK the pad this time.

During the exercise, I thought, "How long do we have to do this?"

Some minutes later, I was running out of breath, when we stopped! "Finally," I thought happily, "FREE-DOM!!!!!!!!!!!"

When we were going back home, mom said, "Well, I guess you were right and I was wrong."

"Exactly!" I thought.

Benefits of Combining Drawings and Subtext to Craft Narratives

Some young writers find themselves "trapped by the linear demands of oral and written language" (Clyde 1994, 28), which must be sequenced meaningfully to make sense to readers. But there is no specific order in which parts of a sketch must be created; and once the images have been preserved, kids seem to be able to organize their thoughts easily. With sketches completed, their stories are there for the telling.

Incorporating sketches and the subtext strategy into the writing process can be powerful! It capitalizes on kids' keen observational skills, encouraging them to examine, record, and interpret gestures, postures, and movement and the meanings they convey.

- Sketching serves as a memory device, prompting kids to remember details they at times struggle to recall. Charlie, a special needs child, reflected, "It showed me what [the event] looked like. I remembered [and] I could write it down."

- The habit of creating subtext brings about a sophisticated understanding of a writer's struggle to consider and address readers' needs; that is, it helps kids "write like a reader" (Smith 1983).

- "When children have opportunities to use multiple forms of communication, they can express different aspects of their meanings" (Rowe 1994, 207). Visual art and the subtext strategy used together are exciting tools, helping even very young writers identify relevant details that support readers' understanding. "Subtext made me think that I should put some more details so the reader can understand what the character is saying in my story," wrote Chizvest, age eight.

- Combining sketches with subtext brings characters—whether imaginary or the kids themselves—to life! This supports kids in making decisions regarding plot as well. "Subtext helped me a lot because I can see how my character thinks and I understand how my character feels," wrote seven-year-old Destini. "It's like a movie. Sometimes subtext is talking to you to put more language [to] give more of a mental picture. You get to think about what you think is going to happen."

When used together as composing tools, visual representations and the subtext strategy help young writers—indeed, *all* writers—identify *what matters* in their stories and, sometimes, which details are irrelevant. Each shift in perspective—from reader to writer to artist to character within the text—provides unique benefits to the learner, enabling the writer to see a piece with fresh eyes. Perhaps seven-year-old Brittney says it best: "Subtext tells me what to put in my piece. It eats up all of the boring stuff and puts better things in. Without subtext, what would a story be—a piece of junk."

CHAPTER 4

Crafting Persuasive Texts

When teachers develop assignments and strategies that sharpen students' sense of audience, the students learn the value of writing as a process of communication.

—Rebecca L. Strange

A "sense of audience . . . is often considered to be a necessary and central characteristic of competent writing" (Smith 1982, 80). Persuasive writing, more than any other genre, requires a particularly keen sense of audience, especially if an author's goal is to move the reader to take action. Persuasive writing requires authors to use a number of strategies to reach readers, including "directly addressing and cueing readers to their expected stance, providing background information readers need, appealing to readers' emotions, circumstances, interests, or sense of humor, and stating and accommodating readers' concerns" (Wollman-Bonilla 2004, 504). Many people mistakenly believe that elementary-age children are incapable of orchestrating such sophisticated considerations.

We've discovered that when kids are invited to use the subtext strategy, which incorporates the familiar sign systems/literacies of art and drama, to step inside intended readers' worlds to imagine their response to the ideas they are proposing, they are able to create thoughtful, well-articulated persuasive writing that can impact readers in powerful ways. Generating subtext for intended readers pushes all kids—even those with limited English proficiency—to establish a desired outcome, to deeply consider the thoughts and feelings of their audience, and further, to plan effective arguments to address anticipated readers' concerns.

From Interest to Action:
Positioning Kids to Change Their World

Laura and her second and third graders had been working on a different-ways-of-knowing unit, studying the effects of pollution on Tacuma Lake, a fictional place that the children steadfastly believed to be real. Together the class read books with environmental themes, such as *The Earth and I* (Asch 1994), *Just a Dream* (Van Allsburg 1990), and *One Child* (Cheng 1999), and everyone was becoming genuinely concerned about the environment.

In a weeklong workshop with a special visiting educator from a local group called Eco-drama, the children had played the parts of visitors from the future who had come back in time to persuade present-day people to change their ways. The workshop had enhanced the children's environmental awareness, but it had ended on a Friday without time for debriefing. So, the following Monday, Laura presented a real reason for a class review: to inform the school's special education resource teacher, who had missed the workshop, about what had happened and all they had learned. She asked the kids to draw themselves involved in an event from the previous week. Discussing their drawn reflections and putting them in order helped the children review and reflect on the week.

After the children shared their drawings, Laura told them, "I want us to think harder about how we were thinking when this was going on, *what* we were thinking, so I'm going to ask you to go back to your drawings and subtext them."

"Yeah!!" several kids cheered.

"You're in that drawing somewhere. Take your sticky notes and write down what you're thinking about as you're in that drawing, doing what you're doing. You can subtext for other people in your drawing, too." The students went happily to work.

When they were finished, they met on the rug. Laura asked them to share their drawings in the order in which the activities occurred during the workshop. A variety of memories and thoughts were revealed, concepts reviewed, and many new questions asked. Two boys even insisted on presenting a short play they had written.

Since drawing and subtexting had worked so well as a tool for reflection and review, Laura and Jean Anne began planning how to use these tools to help the kids write persuasive letters, a state requirement. It seemed a natural next step in their unit on the environment to invite kids to write letters persuading others to support some environmental cause.

Laura held up the book *One Child*, a class favorite, about a child who decides to make a difference and do everything she can to protect her environment—planting a tree, walking to school, cleaning up the yard, marching for animal rights, speaking for the natural world. The author then invites the reader to imagine what might happen if all the children in the world did all that they could.

"We've read this book!" someone called.

"Yes, and we're going to read it again," Laura replied, "because it inspires us. We're going to talk about what *we* can do, how *we* can make a difference. I'm going to ask everyone here to start imagining what we can do to work for change. Now we've all talked about things we can do ourselves—we can reduce, we can reuse, we can recycle—but can we convince someone else?"

Laura reminded them that as visitors from the future in the eco-drama, they had persuaded the people of the present to change their environmental habits and thus change the future. "Now, as ourselves, we are going to try to convince other people to make some changes." Laura reread *One Child*, pausing to discuss sections and to point out similarities between the book's illustrations and those the children had made. When she finished, Katie said, "If we all did what she did, the whole school, we could make a difference in our world."

Katie's comment was the perfect segue. "Now we're going to write letters—we can do this! We can make a difference!" Laura told them. "We're going to write letters to persuade, to ask people to change." She drew a T-chart with columns titled *purpose* and *audience* and brainstormed with the kids, demonstrating with her own request that her favorite Chinese restaurant put its takeout in paper rather than plastic bags and then adding kids' suggestions. Next kids made their own T-charts listing some changes they wanted to see happen and to whom they should direct their requests.

For homework that night Laura sent home a handout she and Jean Anne had devised: "Think about our study of environmental issues and the book *One Child*. Imagine what a difference you can make with your persuasive letter. *Draw* what you would like to see happen as a result of writing and sending your letter." Though they had talked specifically about the intention of and audience for their letters, the homework the kids brought in the next day revealed that their ideas were far too generic and broad. They had pictures of a spotless earth and forests filled with trees nobody ever cut and of factories that emitted no pollutants.

To help kids see that they needed to focus on requests that were actually possible, Laura read *Can I Have a Stegosaurus, Mom? Can I? Please?* (1995), by Lois Grambling, about a boy who provides excellent arguments in support of his request for a stegosaurus. "But," Laura asked the students, "is he very likely to *get* a stegosaurus?" No, of course not, they realized. "So, we need to make our requests for something we have a chance of getting."

Jean Anne, who was videotaping the lessons, had also created a sketch of what she hoped to accomplish and why. She shared her drawing of her neighborhood and the many living things—children, pets, insects, and animals—free from the ill effects of lawn chemicals. In the middle of the page, she had drawn a lawn chemical truck, stamped with the universal "no" symbol (a circle and bar), conveying her desired outcome: "No lawn chemicals in my neighborhood." The kids seemed to understand the task better and went back to work. Then Laura and Jean Anne helped them select issues of their own that would focus their persuasive letters on an achievable goal. This time, the drawings were more realistic, reflecting issues closer to home: the school playground, neighborhood parks, and alleyways.

With the drawings complete, Jean Anne demonstrated how to consider her readers' needs. "We're going to sketch the people we're going to write to," she told the class. She glued the picture of her chemical-free neighborhood onto a larger sheet of paper, creating a border in which she could sketch various members of her intended audience.

Then, thinking out loud as she worked, she sketched and generated subtext for two people she thought would respond loudly and negatively. "I can think of one neighbor who will be very upset at my request," she told the kids as she drew a man with his eyebrows furrowed in disapproval. "He's going to think, *You can't tell me what to do with my property.*" She wrote these words on a sticky note and placed it like a thought bubble above the man's head. "And I have another neighbor who won't like it either, but for a different reason." She sketched a frail, gray-haired lady. "She's elderly and has a big yard. She'll think, *What am I going to do about all these weeds?!*" Jean Anne added the old woman's subtext on a sticky note above her head.

With her readers' subtext in place, Jean Anne planned what she might say in response to their concerns. To highlight this shift in perspective from reader to self, she recorded her responses to their arguments on a different-color sticky note.

Following the demonstration, kids glued the drawings of their own desired outcomes to larger sheets of paper, as Jean Anne had done. As the children sketched their readers, Laura and Jean Anne distributed pads of sticky notes on which they could record these readers' thoughts about their proposals.

As kids began imagining subtext for their readers, many of them discovered that in order to provide a convincing counterargument, they would need to revisit resources for specific facts. Jean Anne demonstrated this as she prepared to argue that what one neighbor does to his property does indeed impact others. "I can't just tell them that I *know* lawn chemicals are bad for the people and the environment," she told the kids. "I'll have to provide evidence." She showed them how to use the Internet to locate relevant information.

So what impact did the familiar tools of drawings and subtext have on Laura's kids' success with persuasive letters? The following are three brief glimpses.

Dznetia

Dzenita, an English language learner recently arrived from Bosnia, was concerned about the trash she had noticed on the school's playground. For her outcome, she drew two neat rows of trash cans on a spotless playground. At the edges of her drawing she sketched two imagined readers, one a bearded man, the other a lady with flowing hair. On her yellow sticky note, she jotted the man's thoughts: *Who will empty the trash cans?* Her lady was thinking, *What if a neighbor uses the trash can?* She addressed these readers' concerns on peach sticky notes. (See Figure 4.1.)

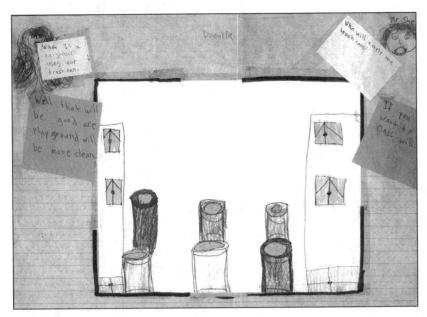

FIGURE 4.1 Nine-year-old Dzenita uses visual art and subtext as tools for planning a letter to convince her principal to take action for their school community.

Her finished letter to the principal shows how she made use of these voices in crafting her argument:

April 16, 2002

Dear Ms. Shrout,

When I go outside I see many pieces of trash flying all over the playground. I see trash stuck to the fence. If we don't have any trash cans we can't throw the trash anywhere because there is no trash cans and some people will throw the trash on the ground. The trash won't stay on our playground. It will go all over the world.

Can we get some trash cans outside? Then the trash won't be flying all over the playground and the trash wont be stuck to the fence and our playground won't be dirty and messy.

You might think who will empty the trash cans. If you don't want to our class will. You might think what if a neighbor uses our trash cans. Well that will be good. Then our neighbor's yard will be more clean.

We really want some trash cans. I think everybody

wants trash cans on the playground so we don't have to throw the trash on the ground. Please will you do this what I wrote.

Sincerely,
Dzenita

Shay-wanna

Shay-wanna, a child from the local neighborhood, had a different audience for her letter. "Mines [sic] is to start putting more garbage cans, like, in the park," she said, her dark eyes serious as she shared her drawing with classmates. "Like, put more than one because there's only one garbage can and it gets all filled up and some people start throwing it on the ground. If we had more than one garbage can in the park we wouldn't have to worry about all the trash on the ground."

One of the readers Shay-wanna drew was supportive. She read his sticky note aloud. *We do need more garbage cans in the park because people dirty it up.* Shay-wanna also provided the subtext for another reader who was thinking about the expense: *How many will you need? You know it costs.*

Shay-wanna's final piece, compelling and filled with her sensitive, compassionate voice, reveals her awareness of her audience's concerns and her thoughtfulness in addressesing them. It also reflects some of what she has learned during the unit of study:

April 29, 2002

Ms. Brigid Sullivan
Director, Metro Parks and Recreations
1297 Trervilian Way
Louisville, KY 40213

Dear Ms. Sullivan,

Imagine a park were kids can play and don't have any worry about stepping on a banana peeling or stepping on a piece of glass. I have, Ms. Sullivan. Each day when my bus passes by the park I see trash on the ground and the garbage can turned over. I think that someone should do something about it and I think that person is you.

Ms. Sullivan you probably think that all of the trash

decomposes but it doesn't. Some of it is plastic and plastic does not decompose but paper and other things can. Ms. Sullivan I have an idea. I think that if you put more than one trash can in the park then we won't have to worry about trash cans overflowing with trash.

You might say that it costs a lot of money to buy more trash cans but it costs more money to hire people to clean it up.

Maybe you are thinking what if a dog knocks it over? Well don't you have the kind that sticks in the ground and stays there?

If you are worried that a kid might knock it over well you can put up a sign that says "Don't kick or push over."

Maybe I could start a little group so me and my friends can start cleaning up the park about 3 days a week.

Well these are my last words to you Ms. Sullivan. Think about all of the kids that could be playing in a clean park if you have the heart to help. The park is on 26th and Broadway down the lane from Pizza Hut. So please do it for all of the children that love to play.

Sincerely,
Shay-wanna
Ms. Wasz Class
Byck Elementary School
2328 Cedar St.
Louisville KY 20212

Making a Difference

When the letters from Laura's students were sent to their adressees, the kids received several phone calls in response. The Director of the Metro Parks Department, to whom Shay-wanna had written, called to thank her for her suggestion. The class heard from the school building maintenance engineer that trash cans for the playground were not practical for an unanticipated reason: they attract bees. Most exciting, representatives from the Department of Waste Management called and said they wanted to visit the classroom, especially to see LaMont and Jacob. When they came, they thanked the boys and told them that the alleys they had written about were being cleaned that day and that their neighborhood would soon have new trash cans.

Imagining Readers in Shelli's Classroom

Inspired by Laura's success with this strategy, Shelli used the same process with her second and third graders. She had been using her daily circle time to discuss current events to help inspire authentic writing for real purposes. One day in particular, Shelli was taken with a television news report detailing the massive numbers of abandoned cars in the city's south end. No one—not even those who called about cars on property owned by the city—was successful in having them removed. A number of city departments were mentioned in the story as those responsible for removing cars. However, spokespersons for each claimed it was another department's responsibility, leaving TV viewers like Shelli frustrated.

When Shelli shared this with her kids, eight-year-old Ja'Quan piped up, "There is a car in the parking lot at *my* apartment!" He described how unsightly and unsafe the vehicle was. "There's a lot of broken glass and drug needles and smelly trash. I saw kids getting in there." Shelli suggested that he research how and why the car should be removed.

After sketching the outcome he hoped to achieve through his letter, Ja'Quan drew his audience—a police officer. In imagining the officer's subtext, Ja'Quan discovered that he would need to know more about the health issues surrounding abandoned cars if he was to be convincing. Once he had jotted down questions, Shelli placed the call for him and asked for the person he needed to speak to before handing the phone to Ja'Quan. He conducted the interview very professionally, reading the questions from his clipboard: *What kind of diseases can abandoned cars cause? What kind of other animals (besides rats) can come? Could you tow the car?* He learned that the health department did not remove cars, but if there was a threat to children's safety, it would increase the likelihood that Ja'Quan would be successful in getting the car out of the parking lot.

When he phoned the police department, Ja'Quan discovered that although they might eventually be responsible for moving the vehicle, he needed to write to another department—"City Call." A true lesson in governmental red tape, Shelli thought.

Shelli got a "City Call" representative on the phone for Ja'Quan, and he explained the problem. He learned that he needed to find out if the car had a license plate so the owner could be contacted and charged for towing. He also got a new address for his letter. When Shelli took the phone to thank the person for helping him, the woman enthusiastically dubbed him "our future little mayor." When Shelli told him this, Ja'Quan beamed and began working furiously on his letter. He made many revisions based on the information he gathered from his phone conversations, and later that day his mom helped him get the license plate number of the vehicle.

JaQuan's anticipation of his audience's needs—arrived at through the use of skecthing and subtext—and his articulate conversations with city representatives apparently made an impression. School had let out for the year and Shelli was cleaning her room when Ja'Quan's mother called to let her know that the car had indeed been removed. Shelli was thrilled that this experience had so empowered a young child who often struggled in school.

Peeling Back the Layers of Effective Persuasive Writing

During her next year of teaching Laura, armed with her new protocol for supporting kids, approached the development of persuasive writing more intentionally. The children were accustomed to using the subtext strategy as readers, so Laura asked them to reconsider a book they had read and talked about together, *William's Doll*, a story about a young boy who more than anything wants a doll of his own.

"In the box in the middle of the page," Laura said, as she distributed pieces of paper blank except for a rectangle in the middle of the bottom half, "draw what William wants to have happen. Then draw the faces of the people in William's life who have something to say about what William wants." Next, Laura asked the kids to imagine subtext for each person they had drawn, writing each one's thoughts about William's having a doll in thought bubbles over their heads.

The next day, after they shared their subtext, Laura asked the kids to take the experience a step further. "Today I would like you to *be* William," she told them. "As William, I want you to read the minds of these people. Imagine what they're thinking. Then use these sticky notes to answer them. Write what you might say to convince them to do what you want." The kids went to work eagerly. Every child knew the story and characters well, so were pretty effortlessly able to experience the *process* of shifting perspectives in order to understand readers' concerns and create their counterarguments.

With their responses to characters' thoughts in place on sticky notes, Laura guided kids once again to become William. "As William, write a letter to your father. Try to convince him to let you have a doll." As a class they quickly reviewed the form of a persuasive letter, and then the kids got started.

Dominique's drawing showed a wide-eyed William gazing happily at his doll. Around the edges he had drawn William's dad, the boy next door, and William's grandmother. To the dad's subtext—*Dolls are for girls. He has a basketball rim what else does he need?*—Dominique had responded, *I want to be a good dad like you.* To the boy next door, who was thinking, *You are a girl. You are a sissy sissy,* Dominique answered, *So you're just jealous.* Dominique had drawn a smiling Grandma thinking, *He's the happiest boy I seen.* Dominique's sticky note reply read, *Thank you Grandma for understanding me for wanting a doll.*

Dominique's ability to step inside the characters, imagine their concerns, and consider how those concerns might be addressed figured prominently in the letter he penned for William:

Dear Father,

   I know I'm a boy and I should be playing with the train and the basketball you gave me and I love to play with those delightful toys, but what I really want is a doll! I want a doll that has blue eyes and a pretty pink dress. I want a doll that has nice shiny chestnut hair and eyelashes that close. I know Grandma understands, and I hope you will understand as much as Grandma understands.

                    Together till the end,
                    William

To give the kids more practice with the persuasive process, Laura used another familiar medium, the Disney film *Cinderella*. Before showing the video, Laura asked the children, "What does Cinderella want? Who doesn't want her to have it? Why?" Almost everyone already knew the answers to these questions so, when the film was over, it was easy for the kids to help as Laura demonstrated drawing Cinderella's dream ball and imagining the objections of her stepmother and stepsisters. Because the kids didn't have to unravel the problem and the characters, energy was devoted to how best to arrange the argument.

When it was time for the students to write their own persuasive letters, Laura again began by asking the kids to make drawings of what they wanted to have happen. Now, instead of drawing and imagining the thoughts of already-existing characters, as they had with *William's Doll* and *Cinderella*, the kids were drawing *their own* requests and would have to come up with *their own* audiences and imagine their subtext. Absent the context of the previous year's lively environmental unit to shape their requests, most of the children's drawings reflected more typical kid desires: a dog, a motorbike, a trampoline, video games. But a few had more serious requests.

Katherine, who hoped to persuade her mom to quit smoking, drew a picture of her mom smiling, holding a healthy baby. Her mother's thought bubble contained a vivid red no-smoking symbol. Having practiced shifting perspectives, Katherine easily moved into the next step in the process, drawing and labeling the potential readers of her letter and imagining reader/audience thoughts—for Mom, Dad, sister, and brother—on yellow sticky notes.

When Laura asked the kids to shift perspective yet again, this time back to themselves, she gave them green sticky notes on which they could jot down counterarguments. Katherine had drawn her father thinking, *She's been smoking since she was 18.* Katherine's reply: *She should still try to quit and she won't live very long.* To her sister's thoughts of, *You know, I used to smoke,* Katherine answered, *But you weren't pregnant and you didn't smoke for a long time.* In response to the subtext she generated for her brother, *I don't think she should [stop smoking],* she wrote, *You should care for her, and you always disagree with me.* (See Figure 4.2.)

It's clear that Katherine's readers are real to her; in her response to her brother, we even get a sense of their relationship. Subtexting helped her carefully lay out her arguments to her mom. Here is her final letter:

> Dear Mom,
>   Do you remember when you didn't smoke and the air was so so clear and you felt a lot better than right now?
> I wish you didn't smoke.

FIGURE 4.2 Katherine's sketch of her outcome, combined with subtext for her family members, helped her anticipate arguments and plan an effective letter.

I want you to quit smoking because it's bad for you, me, and the baby. It's bad for everybody and because nicotine spreads in the air. And the smoke gets in the air too. It clogs your lungs and nose and you will look pale.

Mom I know you might say I don't want to quit smoking. But we would like you to have a healthy baby boy. I know you might be thinking why does she [want] me to quite smoking. I really like it a lot.

I really wish you would quit smoking so you would live longer. And it would be nice to know the baby so please stop. If you stop everybody will be happy for you and the family.

Love,

Katherine

Ailen's request was more typical. An English language learner from Mexico, she wanted a backpack with wheels. She drew her happy self, walking beside flowers, headed to the school bus, pulling a purple backpack with hearts—and wheels.

Ailen drew only her mother, the one person she knew she needed to persuade in order to get the backpack with wheels, looming large above the very middle of her drawing, surrounded by six sticky notes filled with reasons why Ailen shouldn't have a backpack with wheels.

Ailen then jotted responses to each on green sticky notes. When her mother thought, *You already got a backpack without wheels. Why do you need one with wheels?* she wrote, *Mom, it's because that one hurts my shoulders.* Ailen's mother had also thought about seeing a boy trip while pulling a backpack on wheels: *When I forget about that boy that fell down, I will buy you a backpack with wheels.* Ailen's frustration was apparent when she responded, *Mom, you are never going to forget about that boy!* When Ailen imagined her mom's worries that she was going to trip and get hurt, her response revealed that she was able not only to shift perspectives easily between herself and her mother but also present a thoughtful argument: *No, Mom. I promise I am going to be careful and when I am getting on the bus I will carry it in on my shoulders.* (See Figure 4.3.)

In her final draft, Ailen organized her arguments effectively and wrote with a distinctive voice:

Dear Mom,

Do you remember when every time I got home from school and I told you that my shoulders hurt? Can you please buy me a backpack with wheels? The reason why I want a backpack with wheels is because it won't hurt my shoulders when I put a lot of stuff in it and because I like to carry it and they are really, really cool.

Mom, I know you remember that boy who fell down and you think I am going to fall down too. Please can you

FIGURE 4.3 With the goal of her letter clearly established through her sketch, Ailen carefully laid out the arguments she needed to address if she hoped to convince her Mom that she needed a backpack with wheels.

forget about that boy? You saw that he was running. Don't worry. I don't do that. Mom I promise that every time that I am getting on the bus I will carry my backpack on my shoulders. You may say that I already have a backpack, but mom that one really hurts my shoulders.

So mom, could you please buy me a backpack with wheels please, please mom?

Love,
Your daughter Ailen

The Benefits of Using Visual Representations and Subtext in the Service of Social Action

When kids use a familiar form of communication—the visual—to place-hold a desired writing outcome, their drawings turn thought into accessible reality. Sketches give form and substance to ideas, providing a visual draft from which a young author can readily work. Kids not only enjoy this, but most of them, even those with limited written language competencies, can create a successful (for them) drawing!

When kids sketch the individual faces of their audience around the edges of those drawings it somehow makes readers real to them—as if their readers are looking at the drawings, considering the ideas the sketches represent. In creating these faces, children essentially must ask themselves questions about who these people really are, what will move them, what might offend them, and the objections they may have to the ideas the young activists plan to present. Kids' own life experiences are the resources from which their projected readers' personas emerge. Yet this seems nearly effortless for kids, who even as toddlers assign personalities and characteristics to puppets and stuffed animals. While it is important for a writer to understand that there is a living person who will read the piece—the mayor, for example—it is even better if that person is somehow right there, smiling (or frowning) up from the paper, eager to be talked to and listened to.

Once kids have considered what's being said by their intended audience through gesture and facial expression, they seem able to access the thoughts of those readers. Recording those voices—their *readers'* subtext—keeps the audience present as authors consider their own response to anticipated concerns. Students seem to know what to say in response to readers' responses, and they can preserve their ideas on sticky notes. Using different-color notes helps them keep track of whose thoughts are represented. Because kids have worked hard to appreciate their readers' points of view, they are able to develop strong relevant arguments in support of their requests for action. This is in stark contrast to the "nonstrategic begging" (Wollman-Bonilla 2004, 507) that typifies most primary-level "persuasive" writing. In addition, understanding the kind of evidence readers will find compelling pushes students to research what they don't know about the topic or issue, deepening their knowledge.

In essence, sketching members of their intended audience—their readers—and imagining subtext for them creates a deep sense of audience awareness in kids and an understanding of the kinds of relevant details that readers are likely to find convincing.

Wollman-Bonilla (2004) argues that "persuasive communication is central not only to essay writing tests but also to everyday life in a democracy to have one's needs met, to participate politically, to protest inequities, and to convince others to take action. Knowing how to write persuasively provides access to *power*" (510, italics added). When children learn the power of the pen, writing is not just a schoolroom exercise but a strategic resource. We can imagine nothing more thrilling than for our young writers to discover that their words and ideas can change the world.

CHAPTER 5

Revising Multimedia Texts

An effective piece of writing answers a reader's questions, and to do that, the writer must learn to anticipate the reader's concerns.

—Don Murray

In this age of technology, in which images are a part of nearly every form of communication we encounter, the notion of pairing text with images to better convey ideas is naturally appealing to young writers. The subtext strategy can be a powerful tool in producing texts that combine images with print. In a variation of the approach described in Chapter 4 for persuasive texts, kids can offer readers' responses not only to the *ideas* they are proposing but also to *drafts* of the print and visual components of these texts.

Multimedia Texts and Primary-Grade Children

Sandra liked the idea of helping her six- and seven-year-olds create picture books with a software program called RealeWriter (www .realebooks.com), because the text could be shared electronically or printed out. The more she and Jean Anne talked about it, the more convinced they were that the subtext strategy could be integrated into the experience to help kids develop a better sense of audience awareness.

Understanding the increasing need to make every project meet multiple curriculum standards, they designed the project so that the end result would be a multimedia informational piece that (a) supported kids' developing understanding of the writing process; (b) deepened their understanding of the concepts of *purpose* and *audience*, two criteria in the state writing assessment; (c) met core content requirements in another academic area (in this case arts and humanities), and (d) demonstrated learning. And of course, it would provide yet another opportunity to explore the usefulness of the subtext strategy.

Because providing a demonstration is nearly always the first step in anything they teach, Sandra and Jean Anne began their discussion of multimedia books by sharing a wide variety of mostly child-authored samples. They invited the students to examine them and talk about what they noticed and created a chart of the attributes identified. Kids observed that these multimedia publications contained "pictures" (photographs or kids' scanned artwork), that the images frequently matched the words on the page, and that they were sometimes written in two languages.

Examining these products gave kids an idea of *what* they would be creating; but they also needed a demonstration of *how* to create a picture book. Sandra and Jean Anne hadn't yet settled on an overall topic for the demonstration book they would create. During a break, Sandra made her way to the CD player. "We've been studying dance," Sandra told Jean Anne as she sifted through her stack of CDs. "Wait till you see the kids dance." Sandra told the kids to find a safe spot on the rug, pushed Play, and the room came to life. The topic of their sample picture book became immediately apparent: the elements of dance, the text to be accompanied by digital photos taken by Jean Anne of the kids in joyous motion.

The following day, they began by talking about *purpose* and *audience*, elements that were central in assessing state portfolios and are essential in creating any successful text. "One of the things you have to do when you're writing a piece is to think about *why* you want to write it," Sandra reviewed. "You have to think about the *purpose* behind what you're writing." Because the kids' multimedia books would be informational (most RealeBooks are), she linked this discussion to nonfiction texts they knew. She invited the kids to think about why various authors had written their books, nurturing a "reading like a writer" (Smith 1982) habit of mind. After reviewing several familiar texts, the kids were beginning to develop a better understanding of the notion of purpose.

Next Sandra discussed audience. "One of the other things you have to think about when you're creating a piece is your *audience.* You have to ask yourselves, 'Who am I writing this for? Who would I like to read this?' That's your audience." She tried to help kids see that the audience an author chooses for a text influences how she crafts the text, a concept that can be challenging for first and second graders. First, Sandra asked the kids to think about writing for their parents. Then she asked what they might include in a picture book about "living things," a topic they'd been studying: predictably, they talked primarily about content.

Finally Jean Anne asked kids how their writing might change if their audience were different. She asked them to think back to something Corissa had shared earlier: today her sister Chanté was turning four. What if Chanté was their audience? "Talk with your friends. What might you change if you were writing a multimedia book for Chanté?" Sandra and Jean Anne circulated as kids brainstormed at their tables, then invited suggestions. There were some very interesting ideas about how to craft a text for a four-year-old.

Autumn said she would "write about something little," because Chanté was little. Shakiera agreed, proposing kittens as a suitable topic. One of the boys cautioned against writing in cursive—something he was just learning himself—because Chanté wouldn't be able to read it. Seven-year-old Kaira came closest to understanding the point we were trying to make. "It would be different because she's little, and she wouldn't understand the words you were writing if you were writing big words."

Sandra asked the kids to think about the kinds of topics selected by some of their favorite authors and about how they knew when books were written for kids. She explained that the same kind of attention to the purpose and audience of a piece is necessary for any writer.

Creating a Sample Multimedia Book

Confident this discussion had helped clarify the kids' understanding of purpose and audience, Sandra and Jean Anne demonstrated how to get started. By exposing their thinking, they hoped kids would see:

1. How coauthors collaborate.

2. The need to refocus regularly on purpose and audience.

3. The importance of accuracy in an informational text.

Jean Anne told kids she and Sandra were going to write a picture book about dance (they *loved* that!) and that the kids' moms, dads, grandmas, and grandpas would be the audience. She wrote *purpose* at the top of a transparency. "Ms. Hogue and I are going to do some brainstorming, so we'd like you to watch us and we'll talk about what you noticed when we finish. Ms. Hogue, what do we want our readers to think or know? What is our *purpose?* Is our purpose to entertain our readers—to get them thinking about dance? Do we want moms and dads to know that dance is important? Or do we want them to know some *things* about dance, like all of the things dancers have to think about as they move?"

"Well, we don't want moms and dads thinking that all kids do in school is dance," Sandra reflected. "Kids have fun while they're doing it, but we do it because it teaches us what we have to know about the elements of dance."

Soon the transparency was covered with jottings of potential ideas for what to include in the book (concepts Sandra and her kids had been studying):

• Dancers need space and have to be aware of space.

• Music guides the dancer.

• Tempo (speed) influences the kinds of dance one might do.

• Rhythm is keeping the beat.

Jean Anne acknowledged that this brainstorming was a little messy, but that it was an important part of the writing process.

Then she said, "With a RealeBook, you constantly have to check your photographs to be sure that they're good ones and that they convey the right message to your readers." She also compared the photos to the kids' sketches, suggesting that photos might help kids decide what to include in their texts. "Sometimes, when you look at your pictures, it makes you think about things you forgot to include in your book."

Next, Jean Anne placed a transparency of twelve "thumbnail" photos on the overhead projector to demonstrate how to look for those that matched the ideas the book was going to convey. There were lots of giggles as kids recognized themselves. Worried that kids would have trouble choosing the ones that best supported the text, Jean Anne and Sandra explicitly discussed reasons for including or excluding photos. Jean Anne began. "I'm looking at some of these photos, Ms. Hogue, and I'm thinking about our idea of dance as movement." She studied the first photo, which featured a group of kids who had been dancing, but whose feet appeared to be firmly planted on the ground. "If the reader were to look at that photo, they'd say, 'That's dance?' "

"It's a lot to think about," Sandra reflected, "because a photo is frozen and dance is movement."

A photo that showed Hawo standing in the foreground swaying his hips to the music while a train of kids blurred by in the background (see Figure 5.1) sparked interesting conversation. Initially, Sandra was bothered by the blur and wanted to discount the photo, but Jean Anne encouraged her to take another look. "This might be a really good photo to show that sometimes movements are really small, and sometimes they are really big and cover a lot of space. It is almost two things at once. We've got somebody who's making a little bitty movement, and then we've got a whole bunch of people who are blurring past in the background, so it looks

FIGURE 5.1 This photo perfectly conveys two dance concepts at once: *locomotor* and *nonlocomotor* movement.

Dance is all about *movement,* most often to music. And it's the music that seems to speak to dancers' bodies, telling them what to do!

FIGURE 5.2 We used our working draft to demonstrate how to choose photos and text that complement each other.

Others of us are a bit more reserved and tend to move in nonlocomotor ways, snapping fingers, tapping toes, or swaying from side to side.

FIGURE 5.3 Jean Anne and Sandra's multimedia book takes shape.

like they're moving *fast.*" As Jean Anne and Sandra continued this process, kids eagerly joined in. Their suggestions clearly revealed that as a group, the class was capable of selecting photos that supported the purpose.

That evening Sandra and Jean Anne coauthored a draft of their picture book, which they titled *Let's Dance.* The next morning they displayed the page pairs on an overhead projector and invited kids to critique the photos and language. They also talked through the decisions they'd made creating each page (Figure 5.2 is the first page pair of their RealeBook). For pages that had photos without any text except a phrase to placehold content they invited kids to contribute ideas about what to say. The kids were pleased with this working draft and so were we (see Figure 5.3).

Now it was time for the kids to try it for themselves. Since the initial discussion of audience had included four-year-old Chanté and because some of the kids' siblings were in the school's preschool program for four-year-olds, Jean Anne and Sandra specified that group as the kids' audience.

Helping Kids Plan Their Multimedia Books

To help kids clarify the purpose of their picture books, Sandra and Jean Anne guided the class in generating the following list:

Things to Tell Four-Year-Olds About Dance

- It is fun/cool.
- You need space.
- Keep the beat/rhythm.
- Tempo; be on time with the music—fast and slow.
- High/low (level).
- Music makes you want to dance.
- There are different ways to dance.
- Whenever the music is slow, people dance slow.

The list not only helped kids revisit concepts covered in their unit of study but also was an important anchor as they made decisions about what to include in their books.

The next day, Sandra used a variation of Katie Wood Ray's (1999) Organized Inquiry Chart to help kids understand how other authors generate texts for young readers. She provided each group with several texts for beginners, and asked kids to study them. When they regrouped, kids offered observations, along with theories about why the authors had crafted their books as they had:

Things We Notice About Beginning Books	Why We Think Authors Did This
• They have no fabulous words	. . . so kids don't wonder.
• No long or hard words	. . . so they won't have trouble.
• Stories are not long	. . . so the kids won't get sleepy.
	. . . so they don't have to read too much.
• They are very simple	. . . so the kids don't have to read much.
	. . . so they understand.

- Pictures and words match   . . . so the pictures help them read words.

- Each book has eight pages   . . . so kids don't fall asleep.

- They are in a pattern   . . . so if they see the word on another page they still know it.

Given these insightful observations and explicit theories, Sandra and Jean Anne were convinced the young authors were ready to compose.

Let the Drafting Begin

The following day, armed with a lot of basic knowledge—how to navigate the RealeBook software, characteristics of texts for beginning readers, the need to identify purpose and audience, and demonstrations of how to choose photos that support text—the kids became authors, working in four heterogeneous groups of six students each. Included in the mix were four English language learners, three of whom were just days in the country. Although these three students were unable to speak English, they understood the universal language of dance, a form of expression that does not require words.

Sandra provided blank storyboards (part of the RealeWriter software—see www.realebooks.com) and copies of photographs to get them started. Groups revisited the beginning texts and continually consulted the Things We Notice chart, as well as the list of things they wanted their young audience to know about dance. Sandra, Jean Anne, and Sandra's part-time aide, Kathy Fodrey, each guided a group; the fourth group worked fairly independently, consulting teachers as needed.

The room came alive as the coauthors discussed and debated the content of their pieces. Once kids had jotted text on their storyboards, they began choosing photos to accompany their ideas, cutting out and gluing thumbnail photos in place. With drafts complete, everyone gathered on the carpet for whole-class response. "We will listen to each group as they share their draft," Sandra explained. "Then we'll tell them things we like about their draft and any things we wonder about. This feedback will help them make their work better."

One group read:

Let's Dance, Dance, Dance

When you dance . . .

When you dance, you stay with the beat.

When you dance, you do what the song tells you.

When you dance, you can go up or down.

When you dance, you need space.

When you dance, you can make your own music.

Dancing is fun, fun, fun.

"I like that they had a pattern in the book," Kimberly offered. Sandra probed to find out why. "Because that is how some four-year-old books are made."

Nikki noticed the way the coauthors had read their book: "I like the way they sang." Sandra reminded the kids that the coauthors needed feedback about how the book was *written* rather than how they read it. "But maybe it's a good thing that it sounds like singing, because our picture book is about dance and music."

After all the groups had shared, Sandra wondered whether they had noticed the endings of most of the beginning texts they had studied.

That night Sandra and Jean Anne talked about how to help kids reexamine their organizational decisions. The following day they revisited the books for beginners they had used as models, conducting a minilesson to help kids consider how to conclude their texts so they didn't simply grind to a halt. Then the kids returned to their groups to work on more revisions. The project was moving along nicely and the objectives were being met.

Using the Subtext Strategy

Next, Sandra and Jean Anne introduced subtext as a tool for deciding whether their drafts were effective. Sandra asked the kids to sketch a four-year-old boy and girl they knew (or imagined), sketches they would use to help them generate subtext. She reminded the kids that the object was not just to think like these four-year-olds but also to *use* that thinking to make their piece better—to help them *revise*. While some of the drawings bore little resemblance to conventional representations of four-year-olds, it didn't seem to matter. Somehow they still enabled kids mentally to hold on to the faces and needs of young children as they revisited their multimedia manuscripts.

With the images of their readers literally "in hand," the students again gathered as a class to examine their pieces through the eyes of those four-year-olds. As the kids questioned the pieces, they made changes to both text and photographs, revealing a thoughtful consideration of their young audience. Joseph, reacting as the four-year-old he had sketched, offered his subtext for the text "You can dance alone or with a partner": *That looks like fun.* His coauthors Katherine and Katie wondered about the word *partner*. "We put a big word in there," Katherine said. Sandra asked the group what they could do about this. First Katherine shrugged, but then she said, "We can change it." Their final draft read, "You can dance alone or with a friend." Sandra told them, "This is what revision is all about. Having the subtext of the four-year-old helps you make your writing better."

Imagining the subtext of four-year-olds also led authors to revise their photos. One group's text read, "Dancers use the beat." "It really doesn't need the words changed, just the picture," Nathan observed. Others agreed that the photo did not match the text, so Jean Anne displayed all the thumbnail photographs again. Since the group was not satisfied with any of the photos available, Autumn suggested taking a new photo that included hands clapping, hands snapping, and feet stomping. Sandra wondered how they could capture all that in one photo. Jean Anne helped the group brainstorm solutions and took digital photos of each shot they planned. The kids were amazingly fussy. Aaron's suggestion that the shot be taken from "above so we can get up close" was a great one, and Jean Anne finally captured a photo that satisfied them (see Figure 5.4).

Creating subtext also pushed kids to think critically about their choice of words. Ishmael wondered about the phrase, "We dance with joy." "Somebody said we can get a picture that has a smile in it," Brittany explained, revealing that the coauthors had already considered this. Imagining subtext led Aaron to deeper thinking. He argued that four-year-olds might have trouble with the page that read, "When you dance, you stay with the beat." He worried they might confuse *beat* with getting hit on the bottom by an angry parent. "Or," he added, putting his fist up against his chin, "they may be thinking about getting beat up." This discussion led the authors in Katlyn's group to revise their text to read, "When you dance, you stay with the beat of the music" (see Figure 5.5).

As Katlyn's group created more subtext, they realized that more information was needed on their page that said, "When you dance, sometimes you do what the song tells you to do." After discussing

We dance to the beat.

FIGURE 5.4 Many photos were taken and critiqued before kids settled on this one.

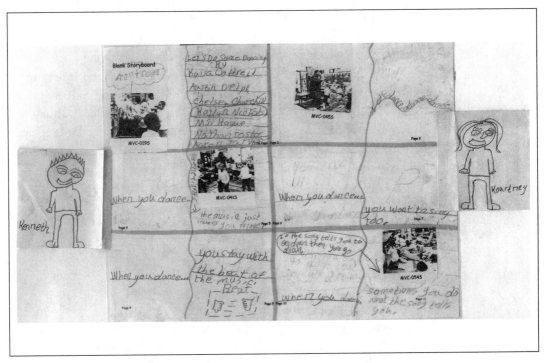

FIGURE 5.5 Note that Katlyn's storyboard, complete with four-year-old readers, contains revisions prompted by her young readers' subtext.

options, she and her group added, "If the song tells you to go down low, you go down." Kids also discussed the placement and appearance of their title: the words side by side, but each larger than the next, or somehow making words "wavy."

Creating subtext for their audience also helped kids celebrate the effectiveness of pages of the text. Kaira was pleased with one group's text for their final page, "Dancing is FUN, FUN, FUN!" "That's really, really, really fine," she said.

Finally, each group composed its own "about the authors" page that included a photo of the coauthors and something about them. As the group Jean Anne was working with reread their draft, they quickly rethought their last sentence, "We put a lot of effort on this book." "Wait!" Brittany exclaimed. "*Effort*." Immediately the group changed their final line to read, "We put a lot of *hard work* into this book," "in case the little kids can't read it," Chase said.

Sandra's kids had successfully generated texts that met the objectives of the project. Their sense of pride was realized when their four-year-old audience came to hear the RealeBooks created just for them. The reading was followed by lively dancing!

When Sandra asked her students how sketching and subtexting for four-year-olds had helped them as writers to create the best piece possible, Aaron said, "It helped me because I thought like a four-year-old." Katlyn agreed: "It helped us because we were looking at them and moving them from page to page. It just helped us to think like them." Nathan said, "It helped us remember that we were thinking like four-year-olds. It helped me remember when I was a preschooler."

fourth Graders Take on Multimedia Texts

While Sandra's kids were using RealeBooks to teach preschoolers about dance, Shelli's fourth graders were creating individual picture books to share new insights about the Lewis and Clark Expedition. In preparation, Shelli had provided a variety of rich learning experiences to help them understand the content. They anchored significant events in a time line of drawings of historical figures that incorporated gestures and facial expressions. They read biographies of Lewis and Clark, York, Sacagewea, and others. They examined informational texts on related topics—including some written by children—and identified how the intended audience affected the writers' choice of language. They also identified the key ideas they thought authors were hoping to convey.

In addition Shelli and Jean Anne took students to two exhibits within walking distance from her downtown school (see Chapter 8).

At one, the kids first studied and sketched a painting that depicted Native Americans and members of the expedition. Next, they created a frozen tableau like the one described in Chapter 1, adding subtext to bring the painting to life. "Becoming" Native Americans and members of the expedition required kids to imagine the emotions, tensions, and fears people were likely to have felt as they met members of cultures never before encountered. As a result, most students walked away with a deeper understanding of the relationship between the natives and Lewis and Clark's party.

Integrating the subtext strategy helped kids make personal connections with abstract historical concepts. At the same time, Shelli used the subtext kids provided to assess their understanding of the significance of the expedition and their progress in meeting mandated social studies standards.

Reading Like a Writer

When Jean Anne joined Shelli in the classroom, she displayed the introduction to a child-authored RealeBook on mammals, asking kids to imagine the kind of visual that would best support the text: "There are mammals all over the world. There are different types of mammals." Ben said he'd have a globe and would put animals around it. Noah said he'd have mammals from different habitats and "put them like a pizza"—fit different slices together. Kristina wanted to show different types of mammals walking around the edge of the earth. "There are all kinds of ways to 'show' with pictures and with words, aren't there?" Jean Anne smiled. She encouraged kids to examine the decisions that authors of the sample RealeBooks had made. She explained that despite their polished appearance, they weren't perfect, and readers had the right to question and wonder.

Thinking Like Readers

Jean Anne then told the kids what she and Sandra were doing to help Sandra's kids create RealeBooks for four-year-olds—things like making lists of "big ideas" and targeting the audience. She asked Shelli's fourth graders to imagine how writing for adults would be different from writing for preschoolers. They mentioned needing "stronger language" that was "interesting." Jean Anne projected enlarged storyboards of the demonstration RealeBook she and Sandra had composed and discussed how they had examined photos with an eye toward conveying their "big ideas" and why they had rejected some of the pictures. She said that since the focus of these fourth graders' publications was historical, they might have to search the Internet or create and scan drawings that would support their readers. After this introduction, Shelli and Jean Anne sent kids home with planning sheets on which to identify "big ideas" and a relevant audience for their picture books.

The students' planning sheets contained a wide variety of ideas. Bethany was going to write about what she liked about the expedition, Kristina about how important sketching and keeping a journal was for members of the expedition. One boy was planning a book on how the expedition members secured food. Brandon had lots of questions about this topic: "Where did they get their food? Did they cook it or eat it raw?" The young author paused, then answered, "Probably raw." Jean Anne suggested he include a question mark beside that point, reminding kids that they had a responsibility to check all facts so they didn't mislead or misinform readers.

Next, the kids created drafts on their storyboards. When they had finished, Jean Anne used the overhead to project the RealeBook on dance she and Sandra had coauthored to demonstrate how to use the subtext strategy to approach revision. She reiterated the audience for their text—parents and family—and began thinking aloud. "I'm going to subtext for a parent." She sketched a female face on a transparency. "What might she be thinking? *Hmmm. About this idea of dance.* She's skeptical. *Why are kids doing dance in school?* On the other hand, there might be a parent with a different view." Jean Anne sketched a male reader. "Maybe this is a dad who thinks, *I like dance. Let's see what they're doing with dance in school.* Let's see what happens if we go through this text and imagine what each of these readers might be thinking about it."

Jean Anne studied the cover of her picture book, then read, " '*Let's Dance,* by Ms. Clyde and Ms. Hogue.' The dad who likes dancing is thinking, *They are having a ball!*" She recorded his subtext on the transparency. Kristina said, "The one that doesn't want the kids dancing is thinking, *They're just acting wild.*" Jean Anne wrote down Kristina's subtext, then added, *Hmph. I'm not convinced.* Ben said, "If I was the lady I would think. *Look at all the monkeys.* That's what my dad says when we're acting wild." Jean Anne continued reading. " 'When you hear the music, you've just *got* to move.' An adult would say, *They can't help it. I think that's what that means.* She returned to the text. 'When you hear the music, you've just got to move. It's almost involuntary.' The skeptic might think, *I'm not sure about that.* 'Try a little experiment and see what happens. Put on some music and see how your body responds.' The skeptic might think, *Well, that's true I do like to tap my toe.*"

Here Shelli contributed more subtext for the skeptic: *I am still not seeing what that has to do with what my kid needs to know in school.*

Jean Anne recorded the suggestion, then continued reading. "'We've discovered that no matter what kind of music you listen to, you just can't sit still.' What do you think the parent who opposes dance will think?"

The students' subtext showed that their view of this skeptic was beginning to soften. Sean said, "*That's true, I have to do something when I hear music.*" Kristina said: "*They can learn from that.*" But Jared was still critical. "*I don't like it because it is cutting into my child's math time.*"

Clay wanted to give voice to the supportive dad: "*I'm glad they're learning that, and I am glad they are dancing.*"

"As a parent I'm thinking, *Kids don't have enough time for PE in school these days,*" Jean Anne said. "This is a point we don't have in our book."

"That would be a good argument," Shelli observed, and the kids agreed.

Jean Anne said, "Sandra and I are going to have some changes to make! There are tons of benefits of dancing, but I don't think they are in our book!" This was all the more remarkable because she and Sandra had already composed a lively draft. This strategy wasn't just for kids!

Creating Subtext for Readers

After being given one last reminder to think like readers, the kids headed back to their drafts to identify, sketch, and subtext for *their* imagined readers. The process was fascinating. Shelli provided sticky notes and asked kids to do as Jean Anne had done: sketch the faces of at least two members of their selected audience (one male, one female), name them, and imagine their subtext. With their readers before them, kids revisited each page of their drafts, becoming those readers as they examined the text (see Figure 5.6).

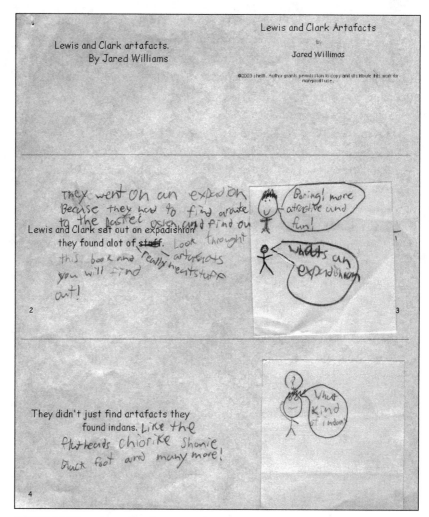

FIGURE 5.6 The subtext Jared's imagined readers offer prompts him to make revisions that really enhance his text.

Immediately they came face to face with problems. "It's making me realize what I left out," Grace observed.

TJ had decided to write a book about animal sightings on the Lewis and Clark Expedition—a potentially interesting topic. But when Jean Anne saw his storyboard, it was apparent that there were significant problems with it. The very first page read: "[Picture of white tailed deer] Lewis and Clark really did find out that his tail was white."

"Who's your audience?" Jean Anne asked. "Ten- to thirteen-year-olds," TJ decided, producing quick sketches of a girl and a boy on a sticky note. "Okay, TJ, let's read your storyboard again, but this time, *be* one of your readers." Jean Anne reread the first page of his text. " 'Picture of a white tailed deer. Lewis and Clark really did find out that his tail was white.' Okay, boy reader, what are you thinking?"

TJ paused for a long moment. *"It kinda makes sense."*

"Write that down," Jean Anne advised, and he did.

"Now—be your girl reader. 'Picture of a white tailed deer. Lewis and Clark really did find out that his tail was white.' What are you thinking, girl reader?" TJ got very quiet, his face looking perplexed. "What are you thinking?" Jean Anne asked again.

"It needs something before this."

"Write that down," said Jean Anne. On the lower half of his sticky note, TJ recorded, *Write something before it.*

TJ's girl reader pointed out for him something that would have been difficult for a teacher to help him see: the absence of an introduction was confusing for readers! Yet with the benefit of his imagined reader's perspective, TJ was somehow able to appreciate the problem.

Benefits of Using the Subtext Strategy to Revise Multimedia Books

The vignette of Sandra's first graders coauthoring RealeBooks demonstrates that even six-year-olds are able to step into their readers' shoes to evaluate and revise their writing. Armed with a clear awareness of potential confusions their audience of four-year-olds might experience, they became active problem solvers, revising their pieces in ways that addressed anticipated concerns of preschoolers. Shelli's fourth graders did the same for their audiences with even more sophistication. Imagining their audience's subtext gives young authors a clear sense of readers' needs, helping them more easily spot gaps in their writing and problems with images they have selected. We see this as a connection between the subtext strategy and Vygotsky's (1978) recognition of the benefits of play. For instance, as TJ stepped into his readers' worlds— imagining their responses to his draft—he seemed able to function in his "zone of proximal development . . . as though he were a head taller than himself" (Vygotsky 1978, 102). And so it was for the rest. What is remarkable is that they did this without benefit of physically present others!

Shelli and Jean Anne asked Shelli's fourth graders what they learned about their readers by sketching them and subtexting for them. Here's what they said:

> "That I could just jump into their mind and know what they're thinking. I thought they would know about wooly mammoth bones, and they didn't." —Caleb

> "I learned I had a good feel for making them. I knew what to write when I knew what they were thinking." —Gina

> "I learned that you should make the writing at the same level as the reader and you should read the reader's mind to see what the reader's level is and what they need to learn." —Ben

> "I learned that by drawing them I became them. Like if I was one of the girls, I would have thought, *Why did they pick Sacagaewa?* Stuff like that." —Cora

> "I learned that some are very picky. They need a pound of information." —Clay

> "I won't always be there to explain." —Eli

> "I learned that I'm not always as clear as I think. Like the seven-year-old I was imagining said, 'What is an expedition?' and 'What is raw?' " —Grace

> "Just because it looks good from my view does not mean it's good because people have other views. Like if I understand it, it does not mean other people understand it." —Jared

> "I learned that my readers have different opinions and I need to reach every one of them. If my reader doesn't believe that my facts are true, I need to back it up and convince them." — Kristina

> "Not all readers want to read it. Not all readers care, but some will read it. For example, one of my readers said, 'Who cares?' Some other people will use it over and over." —Kyle

These responses clearly demonstrate the value of the subtext strategy as a tool for evoking the audience empathy that compels kids to engage in revision. But there are additional benefits as well:

- Challenged to present what they know to an authentic audience, kids have to clarify and organize their understanding of content.

- Kids think deeply about the *purpose* of multimedia texts, not just how to "finish" them.

- The subtext strategy keeps the needs of their readers in the forefront of kids' thinking. This helps them critically evaluate the effectiveness of both their text and their images.

- Creating subtext for their readers enables kids—even first graders—to craft a full, meaningful, multimedia expository text for an authentic purpose and audience.

- The subtext kids offer provides insights into their depth of knowledge of the writing process *and* the content being studied.

Incorporating the subtext strategy into composing multimedia texts motivates even struggling or reluctant writers to try harder, inspiring them to produce texts rich with images and words and that meet their readers' needs. We see this as an essential tool for writers of all ages in the twenty-first century.

CHAPTER 6

Demystifying Standardized Tests

> How do you achieve an authentic fit between reading comprehension and standardized testing? How do you remain true to your strongly held beliefs about how children become literate individuals and still meet the demands of high-stakes testing?
>
> —Barbara Coleman

Barbara Coleman's questions swirled through Sandra's mind as she struggled to cope with the mismatch between formal state assessments and her commitment to helping her kids become thinking literate individuals. Her third-grade classroom was filled with rich literacy experiences in which kids read high-quality texts for real purposes and eagerly entered into conversations about learning. They were hard workers, and most performed above average on daily assignments and formal district qualitative assessments such as the Developmental Reading Assessment (DRA). But in the spring, the kids would be subjected to the California Test of Basic Skills (CTBS), the standardized test our state uses to assess reading, language, and mathematics. New to teaching third grade, Sandra had never seen the test. She was aware of its subject matter and format (and the content and skills required) and had purchased many grade-three "testing practice" books that contained sample tests. But still she worried. How well would these practice tests align with the CTBS?

Sandra decided to begin weekly practice tests after winter break, alternating among math, language, and reading. She hoped the weekly practice tests would build her kids' test stamina and familiarize them with the format and nature of the state test, elements that were still somewhat new to these eight-year-olds.

She soon ran into trouble. It was obvious that these practice exercises were not reaping the benefits she had anticipated. There were significant discrepancies between the kids' performance on day-to-day qualitative assessments and their performance on the "objective" one-right-answer practice tests typical of those they would be taking. For example, Katlyn, a student who performed at the top of her grade group, was receiving scores well below average, some of them failing. Sandra hoped that the problems were temporary, that the discrepancies would fade. But much to her disappointment, they didn't. The kids would moan and cry when they received their latest test scores. Sandra tried comforting them by telling them that she was proud of their efforts and that things would get better; but with little or no change after several weeks, everyone's anxiety mounted.

There was another problem, too. Parents were starting to take notice of these weekly disasters. Although Sandra explained to them that practice tests were just that—*practice*—and were not designed for kids to achieve perfect scores, the parents were panicking and punishing the children for their poor performance. What to do?

During our next teacher research meeting, Shelli and Sandra traded stories about their frustrations as they struggled to achieve balance between what kids needed in order to be successful lifelong learners and what they needed to be successful test takers.

Shelli had been thinking about standardized tests for some time. In the back of her mind, she recalled that Laura had somehow used subtext in relation to testing, and Shelli was convinced that subtext could in some way be valuable. But first she wanted to talk with school colleagues and a state consultant about the racial achievement gap at her school. They all insisted that teachers must teach kids *how* to take a test.

Shelli agreed that failing "to prepare [students] for the reality of high-stakes testing would do them a great disservice" (Mills, O'Keefe, and Jennings 2004, 174), so she began to research what other states were doing to prepare kids for standardized and short-answer tests. She found an abundance of material for teachers of high school students but nothing for elementary teachers. However, the ideas she found did provide some direction. Many educators advocated studying the tests themselves.

Because we'd all had great success with Katie Wood Ray's (1999) "organized inquiry" approach, a simple yet powerful tool for helping learners examine the craft of writing (see Appendix C), Jean Anne suggested we use it to examine standardized tests. She was confident that kids' "noticings" would lead to discoveries about both format and content.

Jean Anne also wondered whether there was a way to integrate the subtext strategy into our study. She created an organized inquiry chart on her laptop, and we gathered around it. "What if instead of asking, *Why might a test maker do that?* we asked, *What was the test maker thinking?*" Jean Anne suggested. "Let's try it and see what happens."

Using a CTBS practice test from a McGraw-Hill test-prep binder that Shelli had brought in, our research team "lived" the same inquiry process Sandra would soon be asking her kids to undertake. Jean Anne suggested we first look at the structure of the test before analyzing specific questions, thinking that this might bring some clarity to the content. The first thing we noticed was boxed directions. Next, we became test makers and tried to create their subtext. We concluded that the intention was to attract kids' attention. We named this obvious feature *direction box,* then listed other places we had seen them. We went on to notice things such as boldface text, the arrangement of items on a page, and the use of white space. Because some of our observations left us somewhat confused, we added a what-do-we-wonder column to the chart we were creating. (See the excerpt in the chart. A template for this chart is found in Appendix C.)

What Do We Notice About Tests?

What do we notice?	What are the test makers thinking? (subtext)	What shall we call it?	Where else have we seen this?	What do we wonder?
Boxed directions	I want test takers to know they'll have to think differently now. I want to alert them to a change in what's being asked.	Direction Box		How does this material differ from text that is not boxed? Why are the questions divided into sets?
Questions in the middle of the text	This will support readers who get lost in longer passages.	Mid-Story Questions		Will the questions at the end be just about part 2?

Hoyt (2005) argues:

> There is a huge difference between test practice and test prepara-
> tion. Test practice happens when teachers pass out reams of practice
> passages and questions that students dutifully complete. Test prepa-
> ration occurs when passages and their corresponding questions are
> carefully analyzed by a team of students while they talk about
> HOW they might navigate the passage and HOW they might
> address the questions. (364)

We had experienced that difference firsthand, and finally we had an idea
of precisely how to support the kids. Having gone through the process
of analyzing the structure of the piece, we felt confident the kids, with
guidance, could do the same—not only for the text structure but its
content as well. Sandra and Shelli left the meeting excited to see how
the kids would respond to the strategy we had devised. They were
confident that this fresh approach would prepare their kids to do well
on tests.

Sandra's Kids Become Test Makers

Sandra launched the test genre study by creating one enormous organized inquiry chart, using one sheet of chart paper for each column. She
gathered her kids around her. "I have noticed that the smartness you
guys display in our classroom is not showing up on the practice tests,"
she began. "Initially I thought, 'Let's just keep practicing and the more
we practice the better things will become.' For some people scores *are*
getting better. But some kids' scores aren't."

Sandra mentioned that she had spent time talking with Jean Anne
and another teacher, her friend Shelli, about the problem, and they had
helped her find a possible solution. Kids would stop *taking* practice tests
and instead take time to notice things *about* them. Then they would try
to think like the test makers and imagine their subtext in order to
understand why the test was constructed as it was.

Sandra explained that they would create an organized inquiry
chart and analyze a sample test, just as they had analyzed samples of
other genres. Instead of asking, "Why might an author do that?" they
would ask, "What was the test maker thinking?" in an effort to get at
the underlying subtext. The kids were comfortable with this approach;
they would just be merging two familiar strategies.

My test Makers name is Becky Navarro. She is women. She is maried. She has 2 kids. Patty Jhon. In her house she has focts paper conters tables and _____ all kinds of She loves her maker. She loves Job as a t Color is black. her hair u She is 6 f

FIGURE 6.1 Elisia's test maker has a life filled with papers, and a head sporting a bun.

Next Sandra gave kids a small piece of unlined paper and asked them to sketch a test maker. She suggested they might think about whether theirs was a man or a woman, what she or he looked like, what this individual would be wearing, even what the test maker's name was. Sandra was hoping that just as sketching readers had helped the kids easily access a variety of perspectives while imagining subtext for invested readers (see Chapter 2), putting a face on the test maker would help kids understand the intentions of this phantomlike person. In fact, kids' sketches proved invaluable, helping them see that real people—who had a lot in common with others they knew—had created these tests. (See Figure 6.1.) Some had kids, some had hobbies, some wore pocket protectors.

Sandra then placed the first page of the sample test (see Figure 6.2) on the overhead and asked kids what they noticed—not about the actual questions or subject of the test but about its *text features,* just as they had done with other organized inquiries. Then, to help kids understand the *intention* behind each decision, Sandra asked them to step into their test maker's shoes—to *become* the test maker. For each thing they noticed, they speculated about what the test maker was thinking as she or he crafted each item, named the feature, and listed other places they had seen it.

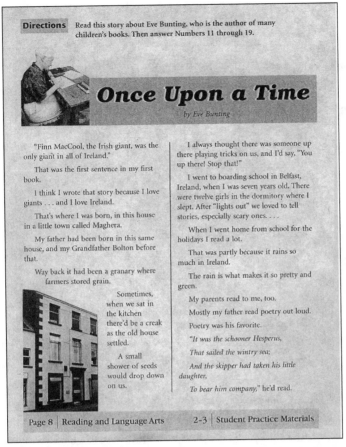

Directions Read this story about Eve Bunting, who is the author of many children's books. Then answer Numbers 11 through 19.

Once Upon a Time
by Eve Bunting

"Finn MacCool, the Irish giant, was the only giant in all of Ireland."

That was the first sentence in my first book.

I think I wrote that story because I love giants . . . and I love Ireland.

That's where I was born, in this house in a little town called Maghera.

My father had been born in this same house, and my Grandfather Bolton before that.

Way back it had been a granary where farmers stored grain.

Sometimes, when we sat in the kitchen there'd be a creak as the old house settled.

A small shower of seeds would drop down on us.

I always thought there was someone up there playing tricks on us, and I'd say, "You up there! Stop that!"

I went to boarding school in Belfast, Ireland, when I was seven years old. There were twelve girls in the dormitory where I slept. After "lights out" we loved to tell stories, especially scary ones. . . .

When I went home from school for the holidays I read a lot.

That was partly because it rains so much in Ireland.

The rain is what makes it so pretty and green.

My parents read to me, too.

Mostly my father read poetry out loud.

Poetry was his favorite.

"It was the schooner Hesperus,

That sailed the wintry sea;

And the skipper had taken his little daughter,

To bear him company," he'd read.

Page 8 | Reading and Language Arts　　2-3 | Student Practice Materials

FIGURE 6.2 Page from sample test that Sandra's students examined.

The first things the kids noticed were the "question number boxes." Then they imagined the test maker's subtext: *I did that so they know how many they've done or need to do. If they don't have question numbers they may skip one and it gets marked wrong.* Additional structural features they noticed included the number of answer choices, the test category, and the page numbers.

However, the most compelling examples weren't about structure but about content. The kids were able to pinpoint the types of questions being asked. They noticed that the answers to some questions were directly stated in the text and that the answers to other questions needed to be inferred from the text. They identified questions about synonyms, letter sounds, and language structure. They imagined the test maker's reasoning: *I made different kinds of questions so they'll get different*

What do we notice?	What is the test-maker thinking? (SUBTEXT)	What shall we call it?	Where else have we seen it?	Wonderings
1. Colums 2. Title in a box in bold at the top in the middle 3. Directions in bold in a box at the top on the left 4. Illustrations 5. Topic Page # 6. Number boxes 7. Questions in bold 8. 4 answer choices	1. They're 3rd graders + they should be getting used to having tests in colums. 2. I want them to know that it's the title + not the reading. 3. We wanted them to know that it was the direction + not part of the reading. 4. we were thinking that we don't want the kids to be bored + just mark any answer so we put illustrations 5. We did that because we wanted the kids taking the test to know that they're about to answer questions with regards to reading + language arts + if a reader wants to look up the same page then they can because the test has the page #, too.	1. Colums 2. Title 3. Direction Box 4. Illustrations 5. Topic + Page # 6. Number boxes 7. questions in bold 8. 4 answer choices	1. Feature articals 2. Feature articals books, scholastic News. 3. on other tests on other papers 4. Feature articals books, scholastic News 5. Scholastic News, on other tests. 6. on other tests 7. Same	

FIGURE 6.3 Katlyn and DeShawn's organized inquiry chart demonstrates that they are noticing elements in this new test similar to those the class had analyzed together.

learning. I asked different questions to get them thinking in different ways. By justifying their decisions as test makers, Sandra's kids were beginning to see the test in a different way. She hoped this would lead to better test results down the road.

Sandra was pleased to have kids thinking deeply about both the structure and content of this practice test; it sure beat suffering through another unsuccessful attempt to pass one! But with the failure of numerous practice exercises deeply etched in their minds, they still seemed to harbor understandable reservations about how this inquiry would help them perform better. While her kids would never have called Sandra crazy to her face, the rolling eyes and groans conveyed that they thought as much. There was a good deal to do before the kids would believe that this process would contribute to their success!

The next day Sandra provided another opportunity for kids to analyze a sample assessment—this time in pairs. As she monitored their work, she was impressed with what she saw happening. Kids seemed comfortable analyzing this new practice test, identifying the same kinds of features they had discussed the day before (see Figure 6.3). And some noticed things—about both the test's features and its content—beyond what the class had noticed as a group the day before. When she asked Kylie and Kirby what the last thing they had noticed was, Kylie responded, "Illustrations," and held up the practice test, pointing to the photos included in the article. "Test makers, tell me why you included photographs," Sandra invited, eager to hear their thinking. Kirby responded, "So the kids won't be confused. Like maybe if they don't know how to do it in their mind." Kirby and Kylie were making a connection to a reading strategy they had used in class: *visualizing* (Harvey and Goudvis 2000). They understood that visualizing was something that good readers do, and as test makers, they were sensitive to the needs of those who struggled with this.

When Sandra asked Jenna to explain her new discoveries, Jenna shared the subtext of the test maker. She talked about what she had named *boxed reading,* a question that contained an excerpt from the reading passage as part of the question. Interestingly, thinking as the test maker, she also included the subtext of the kids who would be taking his test. "I put, *This will remind them of the first time they read it in the story. It will help them say, 'Oh, I know this. I remember reading this at the beginning of the story.'* " She indicated the correct answer from among the four choices.

Feeling confident about the effect the inquiry was having and eager to test the waters, Sandra administered another practice test. She told the kids she wanted to see just how the hard work they had done noticing things about the test and creating a subtext for the test maker would improve their performance. This time the kids seemed eager to prove to the seemingly-present-in-the-room test makers that they could not be outsmarted. Sandra waited nervously for them to finish. She looked over the shoulders of some kids and felt good about what she saw. But she was careful not to get too excited. After they had answered all the questions, the kids even asked Sandra whether they could use highlighters to highlight and label the text features. The mood in the room had changed.

When Sandra graded the tests, she was thrilled. This time most of the kids received higher, passing grades—grades that more closely mirrored their daily performances. Creating subtexts for the test maker had been effective, at least for this practice test. Using subtext within an organized inquiry had allowed kids to demystify the text maker, to make the person real, approachable. In doing so, they seemed also to have demystified the test. Kids had always known the content in question, but earlier it was as if the test makers were hiding what was really being assessed behind heavily tinted glass. The combined strategies had systematically familiarized them with all aspects of the assessment, peeling away layers that had obscured what was being asked. Their real "knowing" was able to shine through.

From then on, Sandra administered far fewer practice tests. Her students had proven what other experts had argued before: numerous repeated practice tests were not the key to doing well on standardized tests; knowing how to *navigate* them was (Coleman 2005; Hoyt 2005). By creating fewer but richer experiences with tests, Sandra had discovered that endless practice was unnecessary.

The Test That Counted

But the question remained: how would kids respond to and perform on the formal standardized test? On the first day Sandra's kids were understandably nervous. They had been through so much and simply wanted it to be over. Shakiera and Courtney were seen bowing their heads in silent prayer. There was nervous laughter and great anticipation: something *big* was about to happen.

Sandra was feeling the same tension, as though she were taking the exam herself. Earlier, she had reassured the kids that the tests were not designed with the expectation that they would be able to answer all questions correctly. She even told them that the "powers that be will show up at the door and ask how you cheated if you get them *all* right." Imagine the horror when, as they double-checked their answers on the first section, kids began to notice they hadn't missed any!

Sandra noticed this too as she walked around the room, but said nothing. Sarah, her face revealing nervousness and fear, finally raised her hand and asked what Sandra suspected everyone was wondering. "What will they do to me if I *do* get them all right?" Sandra had to reassure kids that there was no need to "mess up" intentionally. There would be other, more difficult testing sections and there would be no punishment for getting all questions correct. But what a change in their attitude toward testing! Earlier, Sandra and her third graders had been at the breaking point, nearly paralyzed by thoughts of these assessments. Now their only worry was doing too well.

Stepping Back to Reflect

With the tests behind them but before the results were known, Jean Anne suggested that Sandra use the subtext strategy again, this time as a tool to help kids reflect on the impact of the test genre study. She joined Sandra, who invited kids to think back on their experience. Sandra provided large paper, asking kids to create a box and sketch themselves in it. Most kids drew typical smiling faces, eyes beaming. But when Sandra told them she wanted them, underneath the drawing, to express their thoughts about tests before the genre study, several kids immediately began erasing, replacing the happy expressions with angry countenances. And when she asked them to step back in time and recall what they had been thinking and feeling, the room got very quiet. It was clear that they were *very* reluctant to revisit the experience.

To get them started, Sandra created her own sketch as a demonstration, recording subtext as she talked. "I thought, *I hate seeing the kids so frustrated,* because I could tell, trust me, I could tell. I hate seeing people cry. And I remember people being angry, balling up their papers, wanting to throw them away. That bothered me a whole bunch. But I also had these questions like, *What else can I do? I know I've got to get them ready. Testing is important.*" Then Sandra asked, "How were *you* feeling about testing at that time?"

"You might close your eyes and imagine what happened when Ms. Hogue gave you another practice test," Jean Anne suggested, "or what you were thinking and feeling when you got back a score that wasn't what you'd hoped for."

But reliving their experiences with the practice tests—even for the purpose of reflection—proved incredibly painful for kids. Some who really started to get in touch with their feelings covered their papers as Sandra walked by; she tried to reassure them that what they were feeling was okay. Within a few brief minutes, a remarkable sadness overcame the group. As each child got in touch with those all-too-recent emotions, the writing came quicker and easier.

On the other half of the paper kids recorded their subtext now that the big test was over. Lance's sketch and subtext (see Figure 6.4) captured thoughts expressed by many. It was exciting to learn that so many had been comforted by the test preparation.

FIGURE 6.4 Lance's sketch and subtext show how he felt before and after the genre study.

Results

When the test results were in, Sandra was pleased to see that the scores kids had earned closely matched the quality of their daily work. Their subtext-based organized inquiry had helped them shift from being intimidated to being confident and capable, ready to rise to the occasion. What more could a teacher ask for?

Benefits of Engaging Kids in a Subtext-Infused Organized Inquiry

This process of stepping inside the test maker's shoes not only helps kids to demystify the individual who has crafted the assessment, but also to demystify the test itself! Here's how:

- Sketching and generating histories for imagined test makers helps kids to realize that these individuals are people, with families, hobbies, and experiences like others they know, not some omniscient beings whom they should fear.

- Subtexting for the test maker focuses kids' attention on the *intention* of each test item or organizational feature of the assessment, systematically familiarizing them with the elements of an assessment, peeling away layers of text that can sometimes obscure what is really being asked of them. As a result, kids are able to make connections between the content they have mastered through their day-to-day studies and the items on the test.

Using the subtext strategy to thoughtfully and thoroughly analyze the assessment process replaces the frightening and sometimes traumatic experiences of test-taking with a "can-do" attitude. As a result, kids are better able to navigate through tests and earn scores reflective of their daily level of performance.

CHAPTER 7

Writing on Demand

All thinking, especially all productive thinking, is infused with
feeling. . . . Mind is not separated from affect; affect is part and
parcel of mind. Thus, for the refinement of cognitive skills to be
fully developed, it must in some way be emotionalized.

—Elliot Eisner

By now it is probably clear that the subtext strategy is precisely that—not an activity (though it is delightfully active) but a tool for
clarifying communication between authors and audiences, usable by
both. Imagine our delight to discover that the subtext strategy is empow-
ering and liberating even when applied to timed writing assessments,
which have assigned audiences but are read by another person altogether
—a scorer.

While Sandra was losing sleep over her kids' performance on practice tests, Shelli, who had moved to a new school and was teaching
fourth grade, was experiencing similar fears about state writing assessments. In Kentucky, students in fourth, seventh, and eleventh grades
must submit writing portfolios of their best work in a variety of genres,
written over time. The portfolios are scored holistically, with writers
earning one of four rankings: novice, apprentice, proficient (the state's
minimum goal for all children), or distinguished. But during annual
tests, kids are also assessed via writing on demand. They are asked to

respond to one of two prompts that specify an audience, a situation, and a task or purpose. This assessment is timed, and kids must write independently, without input from other writers or their teachers.

Shelli was committed to approaching the teaching of literacy thoughtfully and creatively, providing a rich learning environment that minimized the pressure of testing. But she was unavoidably concerned about students' scores on the writing-on-demand assessment. As she examined the results for all content areas over the past five years, she discovered that students who were earning scores of proficient and distinguished on their science, reading, and writing portfolios were being ranked as apprentice or novice on the on-demand portion of the state test. These discrepancies were plaguing other teachers as well.

Although critics contend that "writing on demand almost always results in impoverished writing" (Gere, Christenbury, and Sassi 2005, 3), Shelli nevertheless took a hard look at what was expected of kids in order to perform well on the task, then searched for gaps in her literacy workshop. She requested and analyzed state assessment data, discovering that scores *statewide* were lower for this portion of the test. Unlike "real" writing, in which kids identified issues and purposes they found compelling and wrote for audiences they selected, on-demand prompts assigned topics and audiences. Shelli began researching how better to prepare her kids. Nearly everything she found focused on having kids analyze standardized tests as a genre, as Sandra and Jean Anne had already done (see Chapter 6). The single source she found describing writing assessments (Gere, Christenbury, and Sassi 2005) was geared to high school teachers.

Shelli had helped her kids examine the Kentucky's Writing Holistic Scoring Guide (Kentucky Writing Development Teacher's Handbook 2001) and had encouraged them to use it as they analyzed their own writing and provided feedback for others. But she worried that the kids wouldn't think to apply the writing process strategies they were using within the social context of their day-to-day writing workshop to the high-stakes assessment, which they were required to complete without conversing with others.

At one of our research meetings we discussed the topic of test scores. Laura had conducted a short lesson on creating a subtext for the scorer of "open response questions," which require short written responses. Several of us had also used subtext in relation to *invested* readers (see Chapter 2). Asking kids to read a text as another person with a vested interest in the material had helped them make sense of even challenging texts. What if kids approached their own on-demand writing in the same way, using subtext for a *scorer*? Would it help them evaluate their own work? Prompt them to revise?

Deconstructing Writing on Demand

Shelli began her closer investigation of on-demand writing by asking kids what they knew about it. They seemed to be able to *articulate* many key elements of the sample assessments she shared:

- You must choose a prompt.

- You write either a feature article or a persuasive letter.

- You have to choose something you know a lot about.

- Your response has to make sense, have details, and be organized.

- You must have a strong lead.

- You should use "persuasive techniques" (someone's actual words!).

Next, kids observed Shelli as, thinking aloud, she demonstrated how to decide which of the options provided in an on-demand prompt she should select. Afterward, she charted what they had noticed about the process:

- You read both situations and prompts twice.

- You talked out loud about which prompt you knew more about.

- You created a web of ideas related to what you wanted to say.

- You reread the prompt to make sure the items on your graphic organizer addressed the prompt.

Then, in a second think-aloud, Shelli demonstrated how to use the ideas she had generated to compose a first draft that addressed the elements specified in the prompt.

During the next week, Jean Anne joined Shelli to show kids how the subtext strategy could be used with on-demand writing. Believing that multiple demonstrations of complex processes are essential, Jean Anne began by thinking aloud about which option in a prompt to write about. She reiterated what Shelli had already said, stressing that kids should choose the prompt about which they knew the most. "And sometimes, that takes some thinking!" she told them. "I've got to choose a prompt I can really connect to."

The test item, which was admittedly problematic, had been released by the state for student practice. One option required kids to imagine that a friend was having a party and was eager for advice about recipes. The writer was to include a recipe in the letter. Another focused on "random acts of kindness," a phrase about which most kids knew nothing. Jean Anne chose that one, saying, "I like the idea of doing nice things—like the boy in the movie *Pay It Forward*."

"What Jean Anne did just now was tap into her background knowledge," Shelli said, highlighting a strategy she'd been emphasizing. "When she talked about that movie, she pulled out her file drawer of prior experiences. *You* have background knowledge related to your prompt too—so pull it out!"

After quickly reviewing how writers go about organizing their thoughts, everyone (teachers, too) chose a prompt and created a draft. Drafts completed, everyone regrouped so Jean Anne and Shelli could demonstrate the next step in the process: creating a *reader*—the audience specified in the prompt.

"Every prompt has an audience," Jean Anne reminded the kids. "I have to think about who my reader is." She reread her prompt:

> Your school is celebrating Random Acts of Kindness Week. To get everyone involved, teachers and students have been asked to look for articles about nice things others have done, and the effect those kindnesses have had. Think of a time when someone did something for you that was especially kind. Write a feature article about that event to persuade other kids to perform random acts of kindness for someone this week.

She also reiterated the audience for the recipe prompt: a friend. "I'm going to create my own specific readers," Jean Anne continued, "a boy and a girl. I'm going to think about a kid I know, Tyler, who is about your age." She began sketching Tyler's face in the center of the familiar bubble sheet. She jotted notes about him around her sketch as she described him. "He is a neat kid, really shy and quiet, but funny." Jean Anne paused, considering which characteristics of Tyler were most relevant. "Tyler is not likely to approach someone he doesn't know. This makes me think he may not be likely to perform a random act of kindness unless he knows the person."

Next Jean Anne created her second reader, an African American girl named Veronica. She listed qualities about Veronica that were relevant to the prompt: outgoing, caring and compassionate, from a large family. Identifying these characteristics would help Jean Anne imagine what Veronica might find compelling as a reader. "These are pretty different readers," she observed. "I suggest you imagine a person you know as the person you're writing to. If it says write to a friend, pick a real friend."

Now it was the kids' turn. As Shelli and Jean Anne distributed bubble sheets, the kids' enthusiasm was obvious. "*Yes!*" they exclaimed. "We get to do a subtext!"

"Remember, you're creating readers, just like you created invested readers a couple of months ago," Shelli told them.

The following day, after reviewing what students had done thus far, Jean Anne explained that Cody had agreed to let her use his piece as an example. "Cody is writing his piece for Sam, his audience," she told them, then placed Cody's sketch of his reader on the overhead projector. "Cody, would you read the draft of your letter? Let's imagine that Sam has just received it. Read your letter piece by piece, imagine what his response will be, and record his thoughts in the subtext bubbles."

CODY: "Dear Friend. . . ."

JEAN ANNE: What is he thinking about that?

CODY (*a look on his face indicating he has suddenly recognized a problem*): *What is this?*

JEAN ANNE: Why do you think he is wondering that?

CODY: Because he just started reading it. "Here is how to make punch."

JEAN ANNE: What do you think he is wondering about now?

CODY (*stammering as he tries to make sense as Sam*): *This is a response to—I asked him if I knew anything—he's contacting me. . . .*

TACHAE (*noticing that the letter begins without any introduction*): *What kind of recipe is this?* He doesn't know yet, he just opened it up. *Where am I going to find all this stuff?*

SAM (*the friend to whom Cody is writing*): *What kind of punch is this?* because he didn't tell.

JEAN ANNE: Remember, the kid gets this *letter*, not the prompt. And it starts, "Dear Friend. . . ."

SAM: *Who is this from?!*

JEAN ANNE: What occurred to me is, *Who sent this to me and doesn't even put my name on it?* If you got a letter that said, "Dear Friend," what would *you* think?

CODY (*his eyes widening*): *Who the heck sent this?!* (*Sheepishly*) I didn't know who I was writing to.

SARAH: I would be sort of offended.

SHELLI: You identified your audience on the bubble sheet, but you didn't when you composed the letter. Cody, you've helped us learn something!

JEAN ANNE: Let's get back into Sam's shoes again. (*She reads Cody's revised salutation.*) "Dear Sam, Here is how to make punch." Is anyone wondering anything else?

SAM: *What kind of punch? Did I ask for punch?*

BRITTANY: *What is this for?*

ANNA: The letter just starts in without saying anything about, like, "I heard you are trying to make punch for your party."

BRITTANY (*offering another introduction*): "I heard you are having trouble finding some drink for your party."

JEAN ANNE: What Anna and Brittany are doing is offering information so that the reader doesn't take this letter out of the mailbox and read, "Dear Friend, Here is how to make punch." The minute we put a face on the reader—on our *audience*—we start getting a lot more interesting, we add a lot more detail to our writing. And it doesn't look like we're writing for a test.

(*Cody continues to read his piece, including the ingredients for his recipe, one of which is orange juice.*)

VICTORIA: What if he is allergic to orange juice?

BRITTANY: Cody knows Sam and wouldn't give him a recipe that he would be allergic to.

JEAN ANNE: Good point. We are at the end of the letter. What are you wondering?

WILL: *It's about time someone is helping with my party.*

SARA: *I wonder if I would like it.*

VICTORIA: *How long will it take to make it? How long do I have to make it in advance?*

MORGAN: *How long would I blend it? It says what you need and how much but not how many it serves.*

Jean Anne invited some final thoughts about how Cody might close his letter to a friend, and then the kids headed off to their seats, eager to think of subtexts for the readers of their drafts and revise them accordingly. Having incorporated his classmates' suggestions onto his

FIGURE 7.1 Cody values his classmates' suggestions and adds them to his subtext bubble sheet.

bubble sheet (see Figure 7.1), Cody realized he had not imagined an audience of any sort for this piece. His revisions to his original draft (see Figure 7.2), indicate a new awareness of his reader's (Sam's) needs.

As kids finished up their drafts, Jean Anne made her way around the classroom, inviting them to talk about the experience. TaChae artic-

Situation: Your friend is planning a party for his or her birthday. S/he is planning a menu for the guests but is running out of ideas. You know how to make several beverages and foods that would be great for the party.

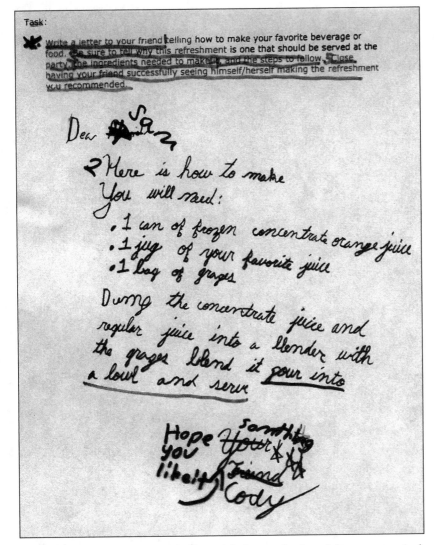

FIGURE 7.2 Cody's revisions to this original draft are reflective of the concerns raised when he and his friends subtexted for Sam, his audience.

ulated some of her struggles in creating a subtext for the readers of her feature article on random acts of kindness. "It's kinda hard, because you have to act like somebody, and you have to really think like your friend. Jasmine already knows how to be nice. All Jerome is thinking about is, *Where did this come from?* There are not a lot of details in his thinking."

When TaChae began to compare her readers to find out why they had made the comments they had, she discovered that readers have different needs. She theorized that Jerome responded as he did because he did not have as many friends as Jasmine, her female reader. In revising her piece, TaChae realized she needed to really work hard to engage Jerome, the less well informed of the two. This decision was important, because it helped ensure that TaChae was likely to convince more readers.

Steven, who chose the recipe option, wrote to and imagined subtext for his cousin, Geno, thinking the two of them could make the recipe together on Saturday. But after Victoria's remark about allergic reactions, he remembered his cousin could not eat nuts, an ingredient in his recipe. Steven's concern about Geno's health revealed that this "practice" test had become much more than that. *It mattered* what ingredients were in the recipe. Steven's ability to personalize the task, to consider these important details, demonstrated *real empathy*—audience awareness. In the end, rather than alter his recipe (because the ingredient was pretty important), Steven selected a different audience—Jeffrey, a friend he knew could actually eat the treat.

The Impact of Imagining Readers' Subtext

After the kids had used their readers' subtext to revise their pieces, Jean Anne and Shelli asked them to complete a written reflection on this question: "How has imagining subtext for your reader (the audience of your piece) affected you so far? Has it caused you to change your piece? How?" When kids had finished, everyone gathered for a discussion.

Morgan began. "Thinking of subtext for my reader helped me realize some details that were missing from my piece. I didn't tell everything I needed to tell, like the ingredients they needed. One thing that was kind of hard was stepping in other people's shoes, like seeing what they are thinking, because you are not them."

Next Sam shared discoveries about his draft. "When I became the reader, I realized I missed quite a few things. Like when I told them to put the mixture in the refrigerator, I didn't tell how long, so I went back and changed it." Sam also said he had trouble reading as a writer. "I didn't really notice it because when I was writing, I already knew it and I thought it was already written down. Then I came back to read it like my reader, and I didn't get it."

"And sometimes we think we have a person we are writing to and we realize we really don't have anyone in mind," Shelli noted.

"You are doing what real writers do, they go back over their writing. They keep trying to think about their readers," Jean Anne said.

Sarah, who had written to her friend Leonard, realized, "He's already had my mom's Rice Crispy treats before, but there were questions about how to make it because he has never made them. It changed how I write, because I don't really look at the reader so much. I am going to try and start doing that. And this will change my writing not just for this prompt, but for other pieces."

Many other students agreed, saying that thinking of subtext for their imagined readers helped them find relevant and important details that were missing from their original drafts. The subtext breathed life into the readers and enabled kids to access thoughts and questions that felt absolutely genuine. The process had converted an inauthentic writing experience into something more akin to real writing. It was as if they were conversing with their readers or participating in an authors' circle (Harste, Short, and Burke 1995) that included the recipient of the piece. These conversations had occurred mentally, with readers' comments preserved in writing for later inspection. An invisible response group like this can be enormously important during a test!

Creating Subtext for the Scorer

Once kids had used their imagined readers' comments to revise their drafts, Jean Anne and Shelli repeated the process, this time asking the students to step into a *scorer's* shoes. First, they helped the kids think about how someone whose job it was to evaluate their piece would react to it. They hoped that the scorer's subtext might help the students tap into the qualities of good writing they seemed aware of in response groups but not while working independently. Hoping to deepen kids' understanding of the Writing Holistic Scoring Guide, the standard a real scorer would use to assess their writing, Jean Anne and Shelli reviewed the language of and criteria for each score, novice through proficient.

Next, they demonstrated how to develop and sketch this new, *uninvested* reader, pulling from what they knew about the qualifications of scorers and the depth of their knowledge about writing. But this time, some students struggled, assigning irrelevant characteristics. As a result, their scorers had little to say that was helpful for revising the work. Once again, the need to be explicit, to show how to consider a

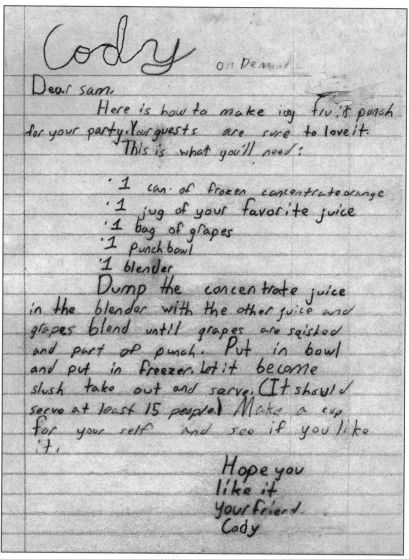

FIGURE 7.3 Cody's second revision, completed after having subtexted for his imagined scorer, shows greater attention to detail. Still, he accurately self-assesses, awarding a score of "apprentice" for this piece.

scorer's attributes and expertise, was apparent. After another demonstration by Shelli, kids began to get the hang of it, to value the scorer as someone who provided a genuine critique of what they'd written.

Revisiting their drafts with the scorer's questions and concerns in hand led kids to still more revisions, this time with a greater focus on the demands of the prompt and qualities of good writing. Cody's sec-

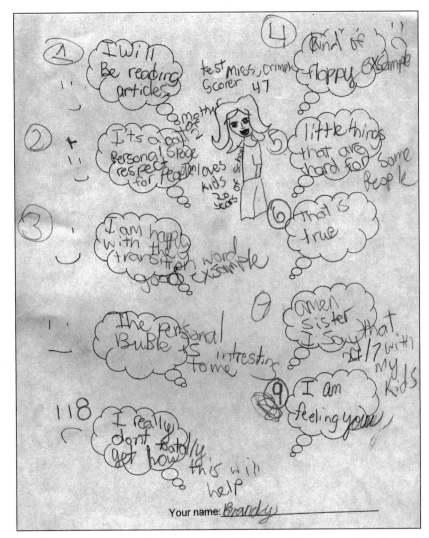

FIGURE 7.4 Brandy's subtext for Ms. Crimple, her scorer, demonstrates that she's accessing qualities of good writing. Ms. Crimple identifies strengths but also indicates where supportive details are "floppy."

ond revision is shown in Figure 7.3. He paid more attention to detail, but (accurately) rated it at the apprentice level.

Brandy had imagined a scorer with two children (her subtext is shown in Figure 7.4), and this information impacted her writing. "Like if it was about a child—you are supposed to put them in a car seat a certain way—she may totally disagree with this because she has two kids." Brandy realized that scorers may have their own personal biases about the *content* of the writing—a sophisticated discovery for a nine-year-old! "Scorer bias" is a very real issue, one that is addressed when educators are trained to score written assessments.

"When I think of a subtext for my scorer and read my piece, it is different than when I read the piece myself," said Morgan. "When I read my piece for myself I'm like, 'Oh—it's fabulous!' Then I read it as a scorer and it stinks."

Over at Last!

But the true test of the benefits of creating subtexts for readers and scorers was how kids did on the state writing-on-demand assessment. After it had been administered, Shelli was on her way to the cafeteria when she was waylaid by her fourth graders. Hugs were interspersed with a barrage of enthusiastic comments: "You were right! That test was easy!" "I did so good! I knew what the test maker was asking!" "I wrote and wrote and wrote the whole time!" "I can't believe how easy that was!" Shelli was stunned; she'd never seen kids so excited about a test they'd taken.

The following week, Shelli and Jean Anne asked kids to write about their experience: "Share your thoughts about the writing-on-demand test you recently completed. Talk about how you did." Fifteen of nineteen kids felt they did well: five were convinced they did "great," four, "very well," four mentioned doing "my best," two thought they did "pretty good," and two, "good." Two even mentioned having "fun" with the assessment! Those who didn't talk about how they did talked instead about how they approached the task. During earlier, presubtext practice sessions, Stephen had consistently submitted lists of unelaborated bullets in response to prompts. His reflection was Shelli and Jean Anne's favorite:

> OH! YEAH I think I did so good. Well, man, I just know that was the best most longest most describiest on-demand I have ever done. This time it seemed easier and also I think I did exactly what the prompt asked for.

Interestingly, without prompting, six kids mentioned the subtext strategy. Tammala, who composed a feature article, attributed her success to the strategy. "I think that I did great, because I used my subtext for my reader and my scorer to help me check myself." Four others mentioned the strategy's usefulness in helping them assess their work and revise. Brittany even found the strategy helpful in *selecting* a prompt:

"I think the on-demand task was complicated. It gave you the two choices, but I couldn't relate to either of them. But when I stepped into the reader's and scorer's shoes, I could. It helped me a lot."

When Shelli and Jean Anne asked specifically how creating a subtext for their *reader* had affected their writing and thinking, Sam wrote, "It showed me a whole new way of seeing things. It is seeing through the reader's eyes and looking at it from a different perspective." Katie was even more explicit:

> The subtext for my audience helps me know what they will read my writing as. I noticed that when my audience read my piece they wouldn't understand it, so I had to go back and change it.

While some kids initially found thinking like the *scorer* somewhat challenging, once they understood how, they seemed better able to assess their work. Theo's reflection was funny but true:

> When I made up a subtext for the scorer I noticed I was looking for ways to subtract points from myself. I guess that's how scorers think: start at four and then go down depending on how many things they have that don't make sense. That's what I was thinking. It helped me fix a lot of stuff!

Brandy was remarkably articulate about what she had discovered:

> I saw things from a different set of eyes because a scorer would have scored in the past and know exactly what she's looking for. She might be able to relate with personal life or have heard the same phrase somewhere else, and see things misplaced in the piece and, honest, they look for every one of those things. You just have to look back and say, "Oh my gosh, I stink." And when you say you stink, it is good because it makes you want to get better.

Leonard revealed his heightened awareness of criteria:

> I had a novice [rating] before we used subtexts. You can really know what the people are thinking and once I did it for the scorer it was even better. I found things I missed and fixed them all and turned it from novice to proficient. Sometimes I will think my piece is really good and will want to turn it in, but once I do subtext there are many mistakes like some stuff might not make sense and even once it said to do a feature article and I did a persuasive letter.

Creating a scorer with relevant qualities requires kids to move beyond simply "talking the talk" of the scoring guide to *applying* that expertise to assess and revise their own work. Interestingly, Shelli's strongest students began to create subtext mentally rather than on paper. They had begun to internalize the strategy:

VICTORIA: Well, when I did subtext for the reader, I was doing it while I was writing because then I would not be erasing five or six times.

WILL: I did subtext, but I didn't write it down. I scanned through my piece and tried to make everything much better. I think the subtext for the scorer made a bigger impact on my piece. Scorers know more about writing, so that makes you think more.

Valuing the Subtext Strategy, Not Just Experiencing It

As kids become accustomed to using the subtext strategy they begin to "own" it and value their own various applications of it.

WILLIAM: The subtext for my audience really affected my writing, and not exactly my thinking. I really changed the way I write my pieces. I put in way more detail. I have really used lots of morsels in my writing because I now have a scoring rubric for a feature article and a persuasive letter. I think about how certain people with certain jobs will react to my pieces.

JORDON: It's like a revising tool. When I use subtext I'm learning and my pieces are being revised. After my first subtext I found so many mistakes I thought that I would use it some more. The truth is we didn't have to use it, but I thought I was better off using it.

In Chapter 2, we told you how fifth grader Michael used the subtext strategy to help his peers better understand him. In the following story, told by Shelli's colleague Caryn Walker, another child uses the subtext strategy as "a tool for social action" (Dozier, Johnston, and Rogers 2006, 19), this time to support a peer who struggles with writing:

I had spent the morning helping kids with their portfolios. I asked Morgan—a very accomplished fourth-grade writer—to work with

Daniel, who's in third grade. Although Daniel has a lot to say, he tends to repeat ideas. He doesn't know how to take things to the next step. They found a quiet spot in the room, and Morgan, who takes things very seriously, grabbed paper and pencils and got right to work. Afterward, I asked Morgan to talk about what she had done.

She said, "Daniel's work didn't make sense. I told him, 'Daniel we need a subtext. This will help you see your mistakes.' I had a piece of notebook paper and made ten bubbles—five on one side and five on the other. I also told him he would learn this in fourth grade so he might as well become an expert now."

In the middle of the page, Morgan had sketched a scorer, adding name and age. Then she had demonstrated reading Daniel's piece as this scorer, putting a number one over the first sentence of his piece and a number one next to the first thought bubble, then writing the score's comments in the bubble. She'd done the same thing for each sentence.

Morgan was definitely imitating what she had seen Shelli do, but she also saw subtext as a valuable tool. She felt that Daniel was going to see how this tool would help improve his writing, and that he would be able to go back and make his writing better. She knew not only because it was demonstrated to her, but also because she had used that technique to make her writing stronger. I'm not sure Daniel completely understood what Morgan was trying to teach him, but isn't Morgan's confidence in the value of the subtext strategy amazing?!

Stepping Back from the Experience

When applied to preparing kids for on-demand assessments, this multi-layered use of the subtext strategy produced compelling results on two levels.

Benefits of Creating Subtext for a Prompt's Specified Audience

- Sketching this reader helps kids use their prior experience to develop reader attributes, to humanize the reader. The subtext helps kids get in touch with their reader's concerns and confusions. Gavin explained, "The subtext helps me know what to write to let the readers know what I'm talking about, and it answers their questions."

- With the readers' comments front and center in thought bubbles, writers seem motivated to revise, inspired by the advice their readers have offered. Theo reflected, "One way subtext helped me was when I missed the point of what my big idea was about. In other words, my supporting details really stink. And the reader's subtext helped me fix that flaw."

- The subtext strategy lets writers consult an imaginary response group during a high-stakes test. Although not physically present, these readers still provide important feedback about the effectiveness of the writing. As William noted, "It's just like a conference." Hailey went into detail about the many ways it helped her: "I found things that did not make sense at all. I found things that needed to go in a different spot and things that didn't need to go in at all. I found things that I would have never found as a writer."

Benefits of Creating Subtext for the Test Scorer

- The scorers' subtext pushes kids to examine the prompt carefully, to see whether they have addressed all the required components. Haley had this insight: "I really found some things that affected my thinking as a writer. First of all, I had to make sure that I convinced the reader to change or do something. Next I had to make sure what I wrote matched the prompt I chose."

- Creating a scorer makes the evaluator real, enabling kids to access their expertise about writing. Tammala explains: "When I step into my scorer's shoes, it makes me come up with different 'ahaas!' because you are not the same reader. It helps me check myself, because it shows me that you just can't be finished with something, write it one time."

- Gere and colleagues (2005) believe that "involving students in actual grading and/or scoring will help them understand more fully the criteria for good writing" (186). In their work with high school students they found that "scoring writing offers a way [for students] to become better readers of teachers' grades and comments as well as to prepare for writing pieces that will be scored by someone they have never met" (187). While this is a critical part of Shelli's writing workshop, it wasn't until her fourth graders created subtexts for scorers that they were able to apply those writing criteria independently. Thinking like a scorer helps kids distance themselves from their own writing and more honestly examine their work in relation to scoring criteria.

- The scorers' subtext helps kids deepen their understanding of the criteria used to evaluate their work.

- The subtext kids offer for scorers is also an informal assessment, providing teachers with important evidence regarding the depth of kids' understanding.

The experience of using the subtext strategy to consider the perspectives of the reader and scorer of on-demand tests helps kids develop a sense of resiliency that enables them to approach such assessments with confidence.

CHAPTER 8

Reaching Everyday Goals

> Our curricula need to take students to the aesthetic end of the continuum as often as possible because "lived" experiences are integrative experiences. As learners, we come to know more fully when our emotions and imaginations are stimulated. We empathize and connect more readily with others when we are wide awake and alive.
>
> —Beth Berghoff

Empathy is at the heart of human understanding. It also fuels the subtext strategy, supporting children as they read and translate human expression. How this empathy is directed depends on our desired outcome: we have only to pick a purpose and adjust the subtext strategy accordingly. The following quick glimpses into other uses of the subtext strategy, each with a different goal, underscore our point that empathy supports the shift in perspective that results in deeper understanding.

Making Connections to Times, Places, and Conflicts

Many kids struggle to relate to historical events, finding it difficult to imagine lives so unlike and far away from their own. Yet, as Elliot Eisner (1998) argues:

Not to be able to get a sense of history, not to be able to stand with Columbus on the deck of the *Santa Maria* and experience the pounding of the vessel by the relentless sea and the excitement of the first sighting of land is to miss—and perhaps even misunder-stand—that aspect of history. And in failing to experience the emotion of such moments, we miss out on an aspect of life that has the potential to inform. (80–81)

The empathy inherent to the subtext strategy is a powerful tool for anchoring even young children in times, places, and conflicts. It enhances their understanding of and appreciation for those living in other times and cultures. As a result, kids seem able to grasp the perspectives of others whose issues and struggles are different from their own. In the following example, kids' new awareness leads beautifully to Laura's ultimate goal: coauthoring a lively and engaging script.

When Laura received a grant to work with Kentucky Shakespeare Festival educator Regan Wann on a project celebrating the bicentennial of the Lewis and Clark Expedition, she and Regan decided to lead thirty-one second and third graders through every step of writing and producing a play about the expedition. First, Laura and Regan immersed the kids in the culture and habits of the period using creative visualization, song, dance, drama, visual art, visits from reenactors, KWL charts, and journals. Just before they were to begin drafting a script, Jean Anne joined Laura and Regan in the classroom. Together, they used the subtext strategy to prompt children to experience a vivid empathy with the characters, the first step in crafting effective, meaningful dialogue.

Laura began with a guided visualization that took kids back in time. They lay quietly, eyes closed, each imagining the scene Laura was describing: a meeting on a river between the Lewis and Clark Expedition and a group of Native Americans. After the visualization, the children shared what they had seen in their mind's eye, solidifying their personal images. Laura then introduced them to Charles M. Russell's 1905 painting *Lewis and Clark on the Lower Columbia* (see Figure 8.1).

"This is a picture that an artist has painted of the scene I took you to today," she told them, projecting a print of the painting onto a large screen. "We're going to look at this artist's idea of what the scene might have looked like when these two boats came together. We can see what this artist thinks these two groups might have been doing, but we don't know what they might have been thinking."

Choosing volunteers to impersonate the people in the painting,

FIGURE 8.1 Charles M. Russell's (1905) painting *Lewis and Clark on the Lower Columbia*.

Laura instructed them to *become* their characters: to assume their positions and prepare to come to life and continue the action, moving and talking as the people they imagined themselves being. "Look very, very carefully at the painting for hints about what each character might be thinking," she told them.

"What can you tell from the way they're holding their bodies?" Jean Anne asked. One child thought they looked crowded. Others commented on the postures of the figures, speculating that those standing were probably the leaders. They concluded that Sacagawea was clearly trying to communicate; they also commented on clothing, boat styles, and facial expressions.

Zatalya observed, "It seems like the one on the team with Sacagawea—the man with the triangle hat— is looking very, very, nervous."

"What made you think he looks nervous?" Jean Anne asked. "What is it about the painting?"

Zatalya replied, "He's looking all serious and he's like, 'Oh, I hope they just don't attack us.' "

"Zatalya, you've already started to think like the character!" Jean Anne's compliment acknowledged that this was precisely what the rest of the volunteers would soon be doing.

The actors carefully assembled themselves into positions that mirrored the painting, sitting and standing in "boats" created out of library chairs. Dakota raised her arms into Sacagawea's pose.

"Look carefully at your character," Laura instructed. "Take yourselves into their role. You are actors. You are becoming this character. That's a boat full of people you have never seen before. You are on this expedition. Here they come in this river toward you, and you are full of thoughts. What actions are taking place? Might they be talking to each other? Might the boat be rocking? Think about what they might be feeling."

"It's like we're making our own script," Joseph piped up.

"That's exactly what we're doing!" Laura smiled. "You are making your own script. Now clear your thoughts, take a deep breath, become your character. When I say action, continue the action of the painting as if it were alive. When I say freeze, stop the action and be ready to tell us what you're thinking." The children's faces were intent, their bodies poised.

"Action!" Laura whispered.

Sacagawea grunted some unintelligible syllables in phrases, attempting to communicate in a native tongue. Her speech initially drew giggles, but she continued unfazed. Those with paddles continued rowing, moving their crafts slowly along the imaginary river. Groups stayed within the confines of their crafts, bunching together like the characters in the painting. A few whispered to one another.

The drama lasted less than a minute, with little actual activity or talking taking place. Had it had any impact at all?

"Okay, freeze," Laura said. "Sacagawea, what are you thinking?"

SACAGAWEA (DAKOTA): *I am worried they might attack us.*

YORK (JOQUAN): *I'm a slave. If they shoot the person who owns me, what do I do?*

A NATIVE AMERICAN (BAILEY): I'm thinking, *Are we going to attack? Who are these people? Why are they dressed so funny?*

LAURA: Keelsman, in the back of the ship?

KEELSMAN (AUSTIN): *Don't hurt us, don't hurt us, please don't hurt us.*

LAURA: Native American in the front of the boat?

NATIVE AMERICAN (CHELSEA): *Who are these people? Where did they come from? Why are they here?*

LAURA: The leader of the expedition, I notice your gun has changed position.

CLARK (JOSEPH): I'm thinking, *I'm getting ready to shoot. Should I shoot the leader or should I shoot one of the men?*

LAURA: Chief?

CHIEF (JAMES): *I'm thinking we should just turn around and go our own way.*

CORPSMAN (SYREETA): *Should we kill these people or give them gifts? What should we do?*

NATIVE AMERICAN IN FRONT ROW (DARIA): I'm getting so nervous because I'm thinking, *Are they really gonna attack us? Why are they here? Why do they have their guns up?*

YORK (JOQUAN): I'm thinking, *Will they be our friend, or will they try to attack us?*

CLARK (JOSEPH): *I think if they attack us, we should attack them back.*

From these subtexts Laura, Regan, and Jean Anne could see that the kids had deeply considered the thoughts, feelings, and motives of these historical figures. When they asked the kids to reflect on the experience, they saw further evidence of the empathy and involvement needed to imagine and sustain the development of a meaningful script. One child debated about whether to "talk to them in English or in another language, like Native American." Another described the challenge of thinking like a historical Native American: "I had to try to experience what a Native American would experience, try to *be* them." Another felt completely swallowed up: "I felt like I was so into it, all I could really think was what I thought the person in the back of the boat was thinking." Even audience members were swept into the scene. "Even though I wasn't down there, I was actually in the time. It felt like I was on the boat with them," one child remarked.

Observing the impact of the subtext strategy on Laura's seven- and eight-year-olds, we can easily imagine the possibilities for helping learners of all ages connect in meaningful ways with historical figures and events, *really* making history come alive!

Dispelling Misconceptions

When Shelli's third and fourth graders began to study the Lewis and Clark Expedition, it became obvious that they had some misconceptions about the relationship between Lewis and Clark's men—the "Corps of Discovery"—and the Native Americans. The Corps' intention was peaceful interaction; they were dedicated to establishing trade routes and discovering resources to share with President Jefferson. But, intrigued by the "Trail of Tears" and some of the battles between early European settlers and Native Americans, Shelli's kids had concluded that the purpose of the expedition was warfare.

To help dispel these misconceptions, Shelli and Jean Anne took the class on a "field study" (Davis 2004), a trip to a special Lewis and Clark exhibit in downtown Louisville that included replicas of the ship, weapons and tools, and animals and plants discovered on the journey. The study began with a guided tour of the museum and a discussion of the people who made the expedition and how these artifacts help us reconstruct their story. The kids then sketched artifacts, answered some guiding questions Shelli and Jean Anne had designed based on the exhibits labels, and wrote down things they wondered about the artifacts.

Next, Shelli and Jean Anne gathered the kids around a historic painting, "Winter at Fort Mandan," and asked them to sketch it while imagining what the people pictured were seeing, thinking, and feeling. As they studied the frigid scene, the students paid particular attention to gestures and facial expressions, as well as the wintry landscape.

After reading the museum's description of the painting, Shelli and Jean Anne invited volunteers to re-create the scene. The actors mirrored their characters' positions. The members of the Corps—Grace, Joey, and Brittany—immediately crossed their arms and began shivering. Brienne, James, and Davonna—the natives pursuing buffalo—assumed a hunter's stance, aiming imaginary bows and arrows. Jean Anne called action, and the painting came to life. Soon afterward, she called freeze, and tapped individual characters, one by one, who then shared their subtext.

JAMES: *I can't wait to get all these buffaloes. I need to get out of the cold and because I need something to eat.*

JEAN ANNE: You need something to eat? And there they are. All those buffalo. And it is freezing out here, isn't it?

JAMES: Yeah.

GRACE: I am thinking, *We need to eat, but we don't have the tools and we are watching the natives. I wish we could have those tools.*

JEAN ANNE (*pointing to Joey*): What are you thinking?

JOEY: *I am wondering if the natives are going to teach me how to use those tools.*

JEAN ANNE: Oh! Brittany?

BRITTANY: *Will they share with us?*

When kids stepped inside the painting, thinking and feeling like the explorers, they suddenly understood why it was necessary for members of the Corps to work *with* the natives rather than battle them if they were to survive the harsh winter. The entire experience—the tour, sketching the artifacts, reading the exhibit labels, recording and discussing things they wondered about, and bringing the painting to life—helped kids tap into their prior knowledge, examine misconceptions, and synthesize their understanding of how the expedition unfolded.

Assessing Comprehension of Literature

At the end of each school day Laura read aloud to her kids. The kids relaxed and settled in, listening dreamily, and Laura was never sure just how much of the stories were getting through. She'd been reading *Because of Winn-Dixie* (DiCamillo 2000) and was hoping to finish it before the movie came out. With the double intention of checking listening comprehension and solidifying and assessing character awareness, Laura asked the children to draw a character from the book and imagine what he or she was thinking—a simple version of "transmediation" (Berghoff, Egawa, Harste, and Hoonan 2000), "taking what is known in one sign system"—language—"and recasting it in another" (3). Completed in less than half an hour, the kids' work offered evidence of their understanding of the book, plus a few surprises.

Eight-year-old Chessara was a small, thin girl with pale skin, and a quick, shy smile. She had a significant learning disability and was still in the earliest stages of literacy. Since Chessara's difficulties were centered on *written* language, Laura examined her drawing with particular interest. The drawing showed Otis and his guitar, being listened to by Opal and a number of animals, including a bird and a snake (see Figure 8.2). Tears are streaming down Otis's face while lines of musical notes, stretching completely across the page, radiate from his head. The thought bubble depicted Otis, tears included, behind bars, under the word *he*.

The drawing convinced Laura that Chessara understood the story. She had depicted the scene in the pet shop, where Otis plays his guitar for the animals. The musical notations evoke the feeling of Otis mesmerizing the animals with his music while also indicating that Chessara

FIGURE 8.2 Chessara's drawing of Otis and his subtext reveal deep insights into the character and his emotions.

was aware of the symbols used to represent music and knew that different symbols represent different sounds. Chessara's subtext—a tearful Otis behind bars—proved she understood that Otis's guitar playing had landed him in jail and that it grieved him to think about it. The written word *he* showed that Otis is thinking about himself, a seemingly small accomplishment, but a triumph for Chessara. Using supporting literacies, Chessara was able to "write" a piece showing that she did, indeed, comprehend the reading in depth, understanding the plot and empathizing deeply with the character.

Pyae, an English language learner from Sri Lanka, was a big, gentle boy who patiently endured being the new kid with no knowledge of English when he joined Laura's class midyear. Naturally intelligent, with a calm, methodical nature, Pyae quickly seemed to understand the English he heard, though he didn't speak much. Laura wondered whether he was following the reading, but when she saw his work (Figure 8.3), there could be no doubt.

While Pyae too used drawing rather than writing to communicate his characters' subtext, his understanding was evident. Otis is thinking about musical notes. Winn-Dixie is running, terrified, from a lightning bolt, the perfect symbol to convey Winn-Dixie's tremendous fear of thunderstorms. Opal is thinking about Gloria Dump's upcoming party, and the food on the table includes the lemonade and big jar of pickles mentioned in the book. Pyae has even shown that Gloria Dump has brown skin, a fact that many children missed. Gertrude, the parrot, is depicted saying, "Dog." Though Pyae might not be able to speak or write in English, it was clear that he understood the story.

The drawings of Laura's native speakers confirmed their understanding of additional characters. Sweetie Pie Thomas was drawn thinking, *I really should stop sucking my knuckle when I'm six*, and, simply, *SIX PINK* (capturing the theme of her upcoming birthday party). A crying Amanda was labeled "pinch faced" and shown to be thinking, *This is yummy, but it makes me remember Carson* (her deceased brother). An ability to shift perspective was evident in one student's drawing of Opal and Winn-Dixie: Opal's subtext, *I want another Litmus Lozenge*; Winn-Dixie's, *I want 700 bones.*

The open-endedness of the subtext strategy allowed more advanced students to expand their thinking. Emily, a bright, eager girl who loved school, used both subtext *and* dialogue with her drawing. She drew Opal thinking, *Does he like it? I wonder,* while at the same time

FIGURE 8.3 Though not accessible through conversation, the depth of Sri Lankan Pyae's understanding of *Because of Winn-Dixie* is clear when he sketches and subtexts for a character of his choosing.

asking her father, "Do you like it?" Opal's father, labeled "Preecher," is saying, "Yes! But it makes me feel sad," while thinking, *It makes me think of Opal's mother* (who had left the family).

Anthony's Otis is thinking about a Litmus Lozenge, too, but this subtext is drawn rather than written. Anthony, a lanky boy with owlish glasses and a fuzzy buzz cut, wrote his name confidently across the page four times. His Otis's Elvis hair and cowboy boots told Laura that Anthony had been listening carefully to the book and had not yet seen any ads for the movie. (The movie Otis has neither cowboy boots nor Elvis hair.) Laura was tickled by the way Anthony communicated that the shy Otis looked down at his feet frequently: he'd drawn arrows from his eyes to his feet.

Through this "reverse" use of the subtext strategy, the kids demonstrated they could visualize the author's words, grasp their meaning, and use a form of visual literacy to communicate that understanding.

Assessing Comprehension of History

Around Thanksgiving each year, Laura devotes three days to a mini-unit on the Pilgrims. The unit centers around the book *Eating the Plates*

(Penner 1997), which details the struggles Pilgrims endured finding and growing enough food to survive. To assess what they were learning, Laura asked her kids to draw the Pilgrims as they were setting foot on land and then imagine their subtext. "What might each of them be thinking?"

Samantha's finished piece depicting exuberant Pilgrims on a tree-lined shore showed she had absorbed important information. Her subtext for one of the children, who had not been allowed to run while on the Mayflower, is: *It is great to play again.* Another is thinking, *I am glad to be off that boat.* Still another: *This place is very pretty.* The child thinking, *I am glad to not drink beer,* may seem outlandish unless you know that no one on the Mayflower drank water. Even the children drank beer. Samantha also drew one of the Pilgrims discovering the stored Indian corn that may have saved their lives. The character is thinking, *Oh I found some food. I think it belongs to the Indians. I will grab as much as I can,* subtext that shows Samantha's awareness of the needs of the Pilgrims and the unwitting involvement of the Native Americans in their survival.

Other kids' subtext reveals similar understanding of, along with empathy for, the Pilgrims:

> *How can we get water?*
> *I wonder how much corn there is?*
> *We need more food and some more water.*
> *Where's the bathroom? It* [the Mayflower] *got no bathroom.*
> *Let's go on the beach to have some fun.*
> *I wish we lived in our own houses.*
> *Let's catch some fish while the kids are playing.*
> *We made it!*

Laura's class had indeed been listening and had developed a basic understanding of the Pilgrim experience.

Confronting Emotions and Sensitive Interpersonal Issues

The subtext strategy can also be an important tool for establishing and maintaining a sense of classroom community. During a field trip to Sunny Acres Farm, two of Sandra's kids had that age-old altercation over who should be first in line. Sandra overheard their discussion but chose to listen, hoping the girls would eventually "treat one another with kindness and respect," a class rule they had all verbally embraced. Finally she intervened, asking each girl to remain where she was at that moment, reminding them that "we are all going to the same place." Jessica, second in line, was less than happy as the perceived loser. "Man, I don't like black people!" she spewed at her African American classmate.

"So—I don't care!" snapped Ashley. "I don't like you either."

Sandra, herself an African American, mustered the calm required to pull Jessica aside, informing her that her comment was inappropriate and unfair. Aware that they were both too upset to have a productive conversation, Sandra told Jessica they would discuss the matter later.

Sandra waited two weeks before convening a special class meeting, giving all parties some distance from the event. During that time, Ashley and Jessica had not become friends, but they were at least civil to each another, and calm—and so was Sandra.

The day before the class meeting, Sandra and Jessica met privately. Sandra explained that they were each going to sketch some of the people affected by the confrontation. Jessica suggested herself, Ashley, two other students, and Sandra, and they both sketched them all. Next, Sandra told Jessica, "Think back to what happened on our field trip. You're going to use subtext to capture the feelings and emotions in the hearts of each of the people we've sketched. I'm going to do the same. Then we'll share."

Sandra and Jessica worked side by side. At one point Jessica peered over at Sandra's paper. "I just want you to imagine and feel what the other people involved might have felt," Sandra said. Jessica seemed reassured that there was no "wrong" way to complete the activity.

After they had finished, Jessica shared first, and Sandra listened without comment or judgment. Jessica's subtext (see Figure 8.4) revealed that she now understood the impact of her comment. Ashley, the student with whom she had had the confrontation, still had hard feelings. Sandra was depicted as a disciplinarian who was nevertheless hurt by the comment. A white student who had witnessed the incident was thinking, *She's mean. I don't like her anymore.* And a student of Korean decent, was thinking, *Hey, she's kinda making fun of me and she's kinda not.* Jessica was beginning to see how offensive her comment was.

Next Sandra shared her own drawing and subtext, hoping to drive home to Jessica the importance of judging people by who they are as people, not by their skin color. As Sandra read the subtext she had generated, Jessica nodded, indicating she did indeed appreciate the feelings of Ashley and other students.

FIGURE 8.4 Jessica's subtext for classmates and her teacher demonstrates an awareness of the impact of her comment.

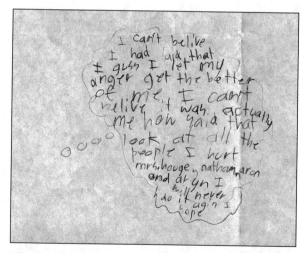

FIGURE 8.5 When Jessica subtexts for herself, her personal growth is evident.

FIGURE 8.6 Breanna's sketch and subtext show that the process can serve as a vehicle though which sensitive topics can be safely explored.

Finally, Sandra asked Jessica to create her own subtext about the incident as she thought back on it: "Using the back of your paper and this subtext thought bubble, capture what's in your heart today as you think about what happened." Jessica's subtext reveals a sense of regret and an understanding of just how hurtful her comments had been (see Figure 8.5).

When Sandra raised the issue at a class meeting, she explained what had happened, but made no mention of who had been involved. Then she asked everyone to think of subtext as she and Jessica had done. The results were profound. While some kids were unaware of Jessica's comment, those who knew about it were eager to voice their thoughts. Their subtext allowed them not only to consider the incident from their own perspective but also to explore it from several of their classmates' points of view (see Figure 8.6). It became clear that everyone understood the importance of treating one another respectfully. Jessica was able to take in her classmates' reactions while her dignity remained intact.

Embracing an Expanded View of Literacy

Beth Berghoff (2001) invites us to "sit in the bedroom of a middle-class teenager and look around at all the 'signs'—photos, books, music CDs, videos, computer games, posters, trophies, baseball cards, model cars, clothes, and a quilt made by a loving grandmother . . . [a collection] of artifacts that can be interpreted in meaningful ways" (76). It *is* an amazing array! "Yet the teenager who sleeps in this room can use only a small portion of these many signs when at school learning, especially in the academic classes of the curriculum. . . . To interact with others and to understand the world, learners need more than just proficiency with language. . . . Literacy needs to be equated with this full range of interpretive abilities, not just the individual's capacity for language." We agree. The six- to ten-year-olds we work with have demonstrated that when they are invited to use multiple forms of literacy, their thinking is supported and extended, their connections and insights sometimes breathtaking.

Sadly, here in the United States in the twenty-first century, the concept of *literacy* is being approached rigidly, restricted primarily to reading, the result of a national effort to "leave no child behind." Yet, ironically, these good intentions are in fact silencing many young voices. "The separation of art from life . . . is a process that often begins when children enter school," writes teacher-researcher Karen Gallas (1994). "And for most children, that separation represents a loss in expressive opportunities at a time of maximum learning potential when they most need to expand, rather than limit, their communication strategies" (116). The impact is even more devastating for children whose first language is not English. "In a multi-linguistic setting, it is especially crucial that students use multiple sign systems such as sports, art, music, and drama to communicate effectively. Students construct culture through these sign systems and are at the same time enriched by them. . . . The more these alternate sign systems become a part of the classroom, the broader the available range of multicultural expression" (Koshewa 2001, 32). Recall what Laura learned when her English language learners used art and subtext to convey their understanding of *Winn-Dixie*. "Literacy itself can be thought of not as limited to what the tongue can articulate but what the mind can grasp," writes Elliot Eisner (2003, 342).

An Invitation

This final collection of stories about the many everyday uses we have found thus far for the subtext strategy is perhaps the cornerstone of our small book about a simple yet powerful technique for helping kids use their "native" abilities to read critically, write reflectively, and think deeply. Compelled by empathy, supported by familiar and comfortable literacies, and energized by the dynamics of play, children can use the subtext strategy to investigate multiple perspectives.

We hope these stories about the many lessons we have learned from taking risks alongside our kids will inspire the teacher-researcher in you to embrace the many talents of your kids. The flexibility of the subtext strategy is an invitation to apply it in your own way, to any situation that requires thoughtful intellectual work. No special talent is required, just a willingness to try and faith in your kids. Their natural abilities to empathize and turn even hard work into enjoyable play guarantee that the subtext strategy will provide satisfying surprises in your classroom.

Appendix A: Subtext Thought-Bubble Sheet

NAME _____

Appendix B:
Trifold Template to Support Young Writers

What happened just *before* the "Uh-Oh" Moment	The "Uh-Oh" Moment	What happened just *after* the "Uh-Oh" Moment

Appendix C: Subtext-Infused "Organized Inquiry" (Ray 1999) Chart

What do we notice?	What are the test makers thinking?	What shall we call it?	Where else have we seen this?	*Our own* wonderings

Appendix D: Lesson Plans

Lesson Plan: Connecting With and Comprehending Fiction

Overview

Children are able to understand the meanings of facial expressions and body gestures almost from birth. By the time they get to school children can "read" a smile or a frown or a hand raised in greeting quite easily. The subtext strategy utilizes this preexisting language by asking children to examine illustrations of characters and the text written about them to imagine their inner thoughts. Children also readily use drama. They play-act often. By asking them to "become" the character, based on the written and visual clues provided in illustrations, the subtext strategy engages empathy and engenders perspective shifting.

By including consideration of the written text and by actually writing characters' thoughts on sticky notes, the subtext strategy scaffolds the transition to written language by encouraging the use of sign systems with which children are already familiar. As a result, students develop more sophisticated inferencing skills and a deeper understanding of character.

Student Objectives

Students will

- Make personal connections to the text.
- Develop increasingly strategic inferencing skills.
- Explore character development and motivation.
- Understand and take on other perspectives.
- Develop a deeper understanding of the text.

Instructional Plan for Introducing the Strategy With an Art Print

Locate a large reproduction of an art piece involving several people with varying expressions. *Birthday Party* by Carmen Lomas Garza (1989) works well.

Session 1—Subtexting
for Characters in a Painting

Procedure

1. Tell the children that when we read a book we have the author's words as well as the illustrator's pictures to help us know what a character is like, but in a painting we must rely on what the artist shows us to get to know a character.

2. Place the reproduction of the art piece where all the children can see it. Point to one figure and ask the children to tell you what they know about that character and say what makes them think so. Do two or three characters.

3. Tell the children that now they are going to try to figure out what each person might be thinking and feeling. "Once again, we have the artist's hints to help us. This time we are going to become these people and act like them so we can understand them better."

4. Pick a group of three or four figures in the painting that have something to do with each other and assign one child to each character. Tell the children that they will become their character and continue to act out the scene in the painting as if it were going on right now. Have each child look very carefully at his or her character and then come up and arrange themselves in the exact same positions as the people in the painting.

5. When the children are posed, tell them that when you say "Action" they are to continue with the conversations and actions that they imagine would be happening. When you say "Freeze," they are to stop in place. When they are frozen you will ask them, "Now what are you thinking? What are you feeling that is beyond what's shown?"

6. Have the children begin, then freeze them. Remind them to "be" the character and speak as the character when they tell what they are thinking and feeling. Encourage the children to assume the characters' facial expressions and body language to guide their interpretations of thoughts and feelings.

7. Repeat this activity until all children who want to have had a turn.

8. As a group, discuss what it felt like to try to be someone else and how the artist's visual information guided thinking.

Session 2—Subtexting for Characters in a Picture Book

It is best to start with picture books written in third person, as they allow children to easily explore several perspectives at once. This strategy is perfect for nearly all stories; but we find it particularly useful when dealing with what we refer to as "tender texts," those containing emotional or sensitive issues. Some of our favorites include:

Be Good to Eddie Lee (Fleming 1997)
Freedom Summer (Wiles 2001)
The Memory String (Bunting 2000)
Now One Foot, Now the Other (dePaola 1981)
Our Gracie Aunt (Woodson 2002)

You will need one copy of the book for every three students and one "big book" copy to use as a model.

Have a pack of sticky notes and a pencil for each child.

Procedure

1. With the children, review the subtext strategy used in the previous session. Ask for student reflections of their experiences. Tell the students that this time they are going to be creating subtext for the characters in a book.

2. Introduce the lesson by sharing a comic strip that features *both* speech bubbles and thought bubbles. Read it with the kids, then invite them to talk about what they notice. Most will notice that speech bubbles and thought bubbles look different. Invite them to speculate about why they might be different, the author's *purpose* for using one versus the other. Clarify that what you'll be doing is creating *thoughts* for the characters in the story you are about to read. Inform kids that these are thoughts that would not be heard by any other characters; these are the "thinking and feeling" that is going on inside characters' heads.

3. Prior to reading the story, take a "picture walk" through the book, inviting observations and predictions. Then read the text aloud, informing kids you are going to read the book straight through once and then come back and think about subtext.

4. Ask the kids to identify the story characters, then ask for volunteers who will "play" the characters as the story is reread. Inform them that you will be one of the main characters to demonstrate what the actors will do.

5. Talk with kids about the setting in which the story opens, and arrange players on your "stage," mirroring what appears in illustrations.

6. Choose a strong reader who will begin rereading the text. As s/he reads, demonstrate how to "think like" your character by *becoming* that character. Interrupt the reading when you wish to share your character's subtext, or to invite other players to offer *their* characters' subtext.

7. Rotate several sets of new actors in, changing every few pages until you are certain that the kids understand how to subtext for characters.

8. Distribute sticky notes to kids and invite them to work in small groups (two to three) generating subtext for characters. You may want to demonstrate using a transparency of a page of the story, and engaging in a think-aloud as you determine what subtext to include in a thought bubble. If working with younger children, you may wish to invite each group to subtext for a single character the first time they experience the strategy. Depending on the size of your class and the number of characters in the story, you may have several groups with the same identity.

9. When kids have finished subtexting, reread the text, picking up a page or two before the kids began subtexting independently. If kids have coauthored subtext, invite one representative for each of the characters to act out the scenes, pausing to invite them to interject the subtext the group has generated as you reread the story.

10. Once kids have had experience subtexting picture books, they seem to easily grasp the idea of subtexting for books without pictures. While conducting read-alouds of chapter books, asking kids to sub-text for characters will help them to think deeply about the story and its characters, pushing them to draw inferences from the text.

Student Assessment and Reflection

Once all groups have shared, ask students to talk about their experience with the subtext strategy. Invite them to reflect on *what they learned* about each of the characters through the experience, how their views have changed. Ask them to draw themselves looking at the subtext they made for the characters in the book. Then they will draw "thought bubbles" that show their new insights about characters. Sharing drawings and reflections should lead to a lively discussion that will reveal the depth of kids' new understandings.

Lesson Plan: Developing Critical Literacy

Overview

In today's world we are bombarded by messages from the media and advertising agencies. As teachers we need to arm our students with life skills that allow them to filter, question, and truly understand the impact of these claims and images. The subtext strategy helps kids see expository and persuasive material differently, from perspectives other than their own.

Student Objectives

• Sketch possible readers of the expository or persuasive piece.

• Use the subtext strategy to shift perspectives while reading the piece, thus appreciating multiple points of view and gaining a deep understanding of the text.

Instructional Plan

Preparation

Select a developmentally appropriate article or advertisement on a topic that lends itself to debate and meets the content standards for your grade level. Make a copy of the piece and a subtext thought-bubble sheet for each student and for the overhead projector.

Instruction and Activities

Session 1: Imagine Potential Readers

1. Give your students a copy of the piece and ask them to read it silently to themselves or with a buddy. (In the early primary grades, you may wish to project a transparency of the material or prepare an enlarged version on chart paper so the class can experience it together.) Ask them to write down their reactions to the piece.

2. Share these reactions as a class so that everyone understands the purpose and content of the piece.

3. Ask students to help you brainstorm other potential readers who would be interested and have an opinion about the piece. List these readers on a transparency as you go along.

4. Choose one of the readers from the list and demonstrate creating a quick sketch of that person in the center of a thought-bubble sheet. Think aloud as you sketch, stepping into this reader's shoes as you describe this new self. *Become* the person you are sketching. For example, if the article is on smoking regulations, you might say: "I am a restaurant manager in my late thirties who's been working for a chain restaurant for eight years. I'm an ex-smoker. . . ." (continue with other relevant details).

5. Hand out the thought-bubble sheets and instruct the learners to select and sketch at least two readers from the brainstormed list. Explicitly ask them to choose readers who are most likely to have opposing opinions about the piece.

6. Have students, in pairs or larger groups, share their sketches and describe their readers. If kids are struggling, invite someone who has grasped the concept to think aloud about her or his new identities.

Session 2: Create Subtext for Invested Readers

1. Remind students how you chose your readers and sketched them based on what you know about them and who they may be. Invite them to recall the readers they identified and sketched yesterday. Share good examples of student work. Give them a minute to look over their sketches and add to them.

2. Explain that subtext is what we say to ourselves, inside our heads. Tell the students that you are going to *become* one of your readers, then think that reader's thoughts aloud—create his or her *subtext*.

3. Begin reading the piece aloud. What are you thinking as this reader? What are your reactions to what you are reading? Think out loud so that kids see how this is done. Write your subtext on a transparency of the thought-bubble sheet as you go along. (Depending on the length of the piece and your students' understanding, demonstrate as much of this reader's subtext as you feel is necessary.)

4. Ask students to return to their seats and choose a couple of their readers. Ask them to reread the piece *as the new reader,* writing their thoughts/reactions to the piece—their readers' subtext—in the thought bubbles on the handout.

5. At an appropriate point, ask the class to reconvene and share what they have done, to be sure everyone is on track.

6. Ask students to color-code, number, or in some other way link the material in the piece with the reader who is offering subtext on that material so everyone will know which reader is reading/reacting to what. (You may want to skip this step in the early primary grades.)

7. After students have created subtexts for their readers, invite them to share those thoughts.

Student Assessment and Reflection

Ask students in grade 3 and above to respond in writing to this question: *What happened when you thought of subtexts for different readers?* (Younger children may sketch themselves and add thought bubbles to show how their thinking has changed.) This will lead to a rich discussion of perspective/point of view and how we read texts differently if we step into another's shoes. Ask students to compare their initial reaction to the piece as themselves with how they reacted to the piece as other readers. How has their opinion about the piece changed? These new insights are likely to lead to a thought provoking debate.

Lesson Plan: Personal Writing

Overview

Personal writing is often the primary focus of instruction for beginning writers. The subtext strategy is a revision tool that helps writers breathe life into their personal pieces. (You can also use this lesson to highlight such things as dialogue, strong verbs, description, and transition words.)

Student Objectives

- Explore topics for a personal narrative focusing on something he or she wishes never happened.

- Use a trifold prewriting planning sheet to sketch the climax or strongest emotional moment of the incident and what happened just before and just after it.

- Use subtext, in groups or independently, to illuminate the emotions in a way that helps the reader feel a part of the piece.

- Make revisions to the draft by integrating the subtext into the piece.

Instructional Plan

Preparation

Before inviting kids to draft a personal writing piece, let them bathe in the personal pieces of others. As you read each text aloud, list things the group notices about it on a chart. Some favorite models follow, but feel free to branch out and use any text that speaks to you or that you think will speak to your students:

> *Alexander and the Horrible, Terrible, Rotten Very Bad Day,* by Judith Viorst
> *One Lucky Girl,* by George Ella Lyon
> *Lester's Dog,* by Karen Hesse
> *Come On, Rain!* by Karen Hesse
> *Owl Moon,* by Jane Yolen
> *Night Train,* by Donald Crews
> *Short Cut,* by Donald Crews

Our Gracie Aunt, by Jacqueline Woodson
Freedom Summer, by Deborah Wiles

Instruction and Activities

Session 1: Brainstorm Topics

1. Invite students to think about a time when they had a very bad day. Invite them to share what happened with a partner or with the group.

2. Tell kids that you too have had bad days but none like Alexander in the story you are about to share. Read *Alexander* and invite kids to discuss some of the troubles he faced. Talk with them about how Alexander almost certainly wishes these things never happened.

3. Thinking aloud, name several things that have happened in your life that you wish never happened.

4. Invite kids to generate their own I-wish-that-never-happened list and share it with friends.

5. Demonstrate narrowing your options to focus on the event that would probably be most interesting for the audience of your personal piece.

6. Once kids have a topic idea of their own, lead them though an oral rehearsal, telling the "story" to friends using the details and wording they feel would captivate the audience.

7. Explain that they will be sketching the big emotional moment of their piece during the next writing session.

While the I-wish-it-never-happened approach narrows writers' choices, it is developmentally appropriate for beginning writers. You can encourage more experienced writers to select seed ideas for a personal piece from their writer's notebook. They are your students—you decide.

Session 2: Prewrite Using the Trifold Planning Sheet

1. Thinking aloud, demonstrate how to use the trifold planning sheet to capture the uh-oh moment of your piece. First, fold a piece of newsprint or chart paper into three sections. In the middle section, sketch the uh-oh moment, the moment when you realized there was big trouble—the something you wish never happened. Then, on the first section of the trifold, sketch what you were doing just before this uh-oh moment. Finally, in the last section, sketch what you were

doing just after the uh–oh moment. (These narrow sketches help beginning writers stay focused on the most important details in the piece while weeding out the irrelevant I-went-to-bed-the-end details.)

2. Give kids trifold paper and have them sketch the uh–oh, just before, and just after moments of their piece. Decide whether kids are on the right track or need redirecting.

3. Allow the kids to share their piece with a partner in a "visual rehearsal," with their sketch in hand.

Session 3: Draft the Piece

1. Revisit the things-we-notice-about-narrative-texts list to remind the students of what good pieces are like.

2. Have kids use their trifold planning sheet to begin to draft their piece. Demonstrate writing your own draft on chart paper or a transparency before the kids begin or at the same time they are writing theirs.

Session 4: Find the Heart of the Piece

1. Remind students that good writers revisit their pieces to ensure that their piece meets the needs of their readers.

2. Return to your sketches and demonstrate how you would create subtext for the people involved in the event. Begin with the uh–oh moment. On a sticky note write down what you (and anyone else in the sketch) thought and wondered. Do the same with the just-before and just-after sketches, for everyone in them.

3. Invite kids to discuss what they noticed during your demonstration.

4. Arm kids with sticky notes and send them off to create subtext for themselves and the other people in their sketches. They may work independently or in groups (working in groups, they have the benefit of subtext ideas generated by the other members).

5. Invite the kids to think about where the subtext might fit in their draft.

Session 5: Add Subtext

1. Revisit the things-we-notice-about-narrative-texts list, the trifold planning sheets, and the previously created subtexts.

2. Demonstrate how you might take the subtext you created and incorporate it into your piece.

3. Invite the kids to return to their piece to do the same.

4. Ask kids to share their revised piece with their group and invite feedback on the changes they've made.

Celebrating Authorship

Host some form of celebration after all the pieces are completed: an "open mike," a writer's roundtable, and classroom or school publications are a few of many possibilities. The format is not as important as allowing the kids to celebrate their hard work with a real audience, not just you as their teacher.

Student Assessment and Reflection

Invite kids to reflect on what they know now about writing personal pieces that they did not know before this experience. This can be done in a letter to you, an open-ended reflection, or a class discussion. Use your state's scoring guide or other prescribed criteria to assess the level of proficiency in each piece. This will let you know what is going well in your writing program and where to go from here.

Lesson Plan: Crafting Persuasive Texts

Overview

Many educators feel that young children are incapable of writing convincing persuasive pieces, the kind we use to take social action. However, by using sketches to preserve the action they hope to accomplish through their writing and creating a subtext for their intended audience, they are able not only to identify readers' potential objections but also to use those insights to plan compelling pieces. After this introductory lesson, kids can move on to draft more personal pieces to accomplish real-world goals.

Student Objectives

- Watch the film *Cinderella,* focusing on Cinderella's desire to go to the ball and her persuasive efforts to get there.

- Draw Cinderella's desired outcome.

- Draw the faces of the people Cinderella needs to persuade to let her attend the ball.

- Record on sticky notes the objections of each of the members of Cinderella's audience (their subtext).

- Respond to these objections on sticky notes.

- Help draft a group-written persuasive letter from Cinderella.

Instructional Plan

Preparation

Acquire a copy of the animated Disney movie *Cinderella*. Prepare blank paper for students in two sizes. Prepare blank paper for your demonstration in two sizes (the same size as the kids' or larger if you wish).

Session 1: Anticipate Opposing Arguments

1. Tell the students they are going to watch the film *Cinderella*. Afterward they will draw, write about, and discuss answers to the following questions: *What does Cinderella want? Who doesn't want her to have it? Why?*

2. Watch the film.

3. Ask, "What does Cinderella want?" As the children answer, use your smaller piece of paper to draw Cinderella happily dancing at the ball, her desired outcome. Use a glue stick to place your drawing in the bottom middle of your larger piece of paper.

4. Ask, "Who doesn't want Cinderella to have what she wants?" As the children respond, ask them to describe these characters (especially their expressions) so that you can draw their faces in the border around the drawing of Cinderella at the ball.

5. Say, "Now what do you imagine these people I've drawn—Cinderella's stepmother and stepsisters—think about Cinderella wanting to go to the ball?"

6. Write each character's thoughts on the same color sticky notes and place them above the appropriate sketch.

7. Ask, "What could Cinderella say to argue with them? How could she persuade them to let her go to the ball?" Write these responses on different color sticky notes and place them next to the objections they are refuting.

8. As a class, use the objections of Cinderella's audience and Cinderella's counterarguments to compose a persuasive letter from Cinderella to her stepfamily asking to be allowed to go to the ball.

Sessions 2 and 3: Developing Personal Desired Outcomes

1. Give the following homework assignment: "Draw a picture of something you would like to see happen." Tell the children that their request should be for something that really could occur. If appropriate, connect their thinking to a unit of study. Demonstrate by sketching your own desired outcome as you talk about what you're thinking.

2. When the homework is returned the following day, ask each child to show their drawing and explain what it is they want to have happen. (If the homework comes back with requests that are too broad or unrealistic, try reading and discussing *Mom, Can I Have a Stegosaurus?* (Grambling 1995) then reassigning the homework to get more reasonable requests.)

3. Draw your own desired outcome again on a piece of white 9 x 12 construction paper, pointing out any new details or insights.

4. After checking for appropriateness, have each child redraw their own requests on construction paper like yours.

5. Call the children back together to share their drawings.

6. Tell them that in the next session they will be drawing the faces of the people they will have to persuade in order to get what they want. (You may want to make this a homework assignment to give them time to consider who these people might be.)

Session 4: Establishing Audience and Anticipating Arguments

1. With the children watching, glue your desired outcome drawing onto the bottom center of a bigger piece of construction paper (18" x 24").

2. Brainstorm with the children about who might be against your idea and what those readers might look like. Draw each face around the edges of your desired outcome drawing.

3. Using yellow sticky notes, write what each person who opposes your idea might be thinking.

4. Give each child a large piece of paper and a glue stick. Have them glue down their drawings from the last session like you did and sub-text their audience's thoughts.

5. Share.

Session 5: Developing Counterargument

1. Using a different-colored sticky note, demonstrate with your piece what you might say in response to each of your reader's objections or concerns.

2. Give the children the second color of sticky note and have them respond to their audience members' subtext.

Session 6: Beginning the Persuasive Letter

1. Gather the children and display your piece (desired outcome drawing surrounded by sketches of audience faces, subtext of audience, and your responding arguments).

2. Tell the children that it is now time to begin to draft their persuasive letters. Remind them to decide which of their audience members they really want to write to.

3. Develop your lead and first paragraph by examining and describing your drawing of what you want to happen. (Depending upon the age and skill of your students, you may want to stop and have them draft this part of their own letters before continuing.)

4. Demonstrate how to develop subsequent paragraphs, continually revisiting the anticipated objections of your audience and then answering them with your counterargument.

5. Invite the children to begin drafting their own persuasive letters.

6. With drafts complete, engage the kids in conferencing in pairs or small groups.

7. Model the closing paragraph by once again restating the benefits of your outcome being fulfilled and thanking the reader for his/her time.

8. Continue the writing process with additional conferencing, revising, and editing (including helping each child find an actual address to which to send their letter) until a satisfying letter is produced.

9. Send the letters! Without mailing letters to a real audience, this experience becomes nothing more than a school exercise. But if mailed, there is the possibility that kids can see that they can impact their world in positive and powerful ways!

Student Assessment and Reflection

Ask students to draw the addressee opening their letter, and subtext what he or she is thinking. Using these drawings as a springboard, discuss the effectiveness of their letters with the children asking why they do or do not believe their requests will be granted. Invite them to articulate specific "pluses" about their letters. Then ask them to identify what they could have done differently to improve the likelihood that their letters would have had a powerful impact on their readers.

Lesson Plan: Writing and Revising Multimedia Texts

Overview

One of the greatest challenges for writers of all ages, especially those who are new to writing, is developing a sense of audience awareness—anticipating how readers will receive and respond to their texts. This lesson uses the subtext strategy as a tool for revision, enabling writers to step inside their readers' hearts and minds to understand and predict where readers may connect or struggle with the text being created. It combines core content, technology, and the writing process to support kids as they produce multimedia texts called RealeBooks (Condon and McGuffee 2001) using free RealeWriter software (go to www .realebook.com).

Student Objectives

- Create a multimedia nonfiction text for a clear purpose and specific audience.

- Capture images that help convey meaning to readers.

- Use a storyboard to plan the layout and text of a RealeBook.

- Use the subtext strategy to anticipate readers' needs and make revisions based on those needs.

- Share the final draft of the RealeBook with the intended audience.

Instructional Plan

Preparation

Think about recent units of study and select one that lends itself to the creation of a nonfiction piece. *It is extremely helpful if someone has captured digital images of the work done as part of the unit.* As a class, create or revisit an anchor chart that features the big ideas from the unit. Distribute several RealeBooks to the class and invite students to explore them. (A chart listing the things they notice will come in handy when the kids begin crafting their own books.)

Instruction and Activities

This is a long-term project. You may work for a period of consecutive days until it is complete or spread it out over two or three weeks with breaks between sessions.

Session 1: Establish a Clear Purpose and Audience

1. Review the anchor chart from a recent unit of study.

2. Display a RealeBook and explain the objectives of this project.

3. Lead a discussion about purpose and audience, clearly defining these terms and demonstrating how they affect one's writing. Decide on a purpose and audience for the RealeBook project.

4. Chart the important things the class wants to share with the audience they have selected.

5. Gather samples of pieces written for a similar audience and begin to explore what other writers have done in crafting these pieces.

6. Chart the discoveries on a things-we-notice chart, inviting kids to speculate why authors made the decisions they did.

Session 2: Use a Storyboard to Generate a Draft

1. Review all anchor charts—(a) big ideas from the unit, (b) features of RealeBooks, (c) things authors of comparable texts have done.

2. Review the purpose and audience for the RealeBook.

3. Demonstrate how to use a storyboard to generate a draft of the text that meets the outlined objectives.

4. Invite the kids to create their own storyboards. (Working in pairs or small groups at first is probably a good idea.)

Session 3: Capture and/or Re-create Images That Support the Text

1. Explain how picture books use words and pictures to carry meaning, and demonstrate how you would use a digital camera or the Internet to capture images that support a text.

2. Explicitly remind kids that words and pictures/illustrations usually match.

3. Ask students to select photos for their piece from the images captured during the unit.

4. Invite kids to use a digital camera to plan and capture additional images that support the ideas in their pieces.

Session 4: Sketch and Create Subtext for Readers

1. Review the purpose of and audience for the piece.

2. Invite kids to sketch members of their audience.

3. Using your own draft and sketches, think aloud as you become someone else reading your piece. Stop on each page and create your reader's subtext—share things you as the reader like, things you wonder about, points of confusion. Write this subtext on sticky notes alongside the text.

4. Ask your students to read their drafts as one of their readers and capture the subtext on sticky notes.

Session 5: Revise the RealeBooks

1. Demonstrate using your reader's subtext to make changes in the piece to meet the reader's needs.

2. Ask kids to revise their RealeBooks based on their reader's subtext.

3. Have kids share their work in response groups so that they receive additional feedback about the effectiveness of their draft.

4. Invite them to make any additional revisions necessary to firm up the piece. (The piece is now ready for editing.)

Session 6: Head for the Computer!

1. Demonstrate how to use the RealeWriter software.

2. Have students input their pieces on the computer.

3. Ask them to print and assemble their pieces.

4. Celebrate by having students share their pieces with the intended audience.

5. Post RealeBooks on your class webpage or school website!

Student Assessment and Reflection

Ask kids to reflect in writing on what they know about writing now that they did not know before the project began. (You may first wish to review the objectives of the project and the process used to generate the piece.) Use these reflections to assess your writers' growth.

Lesson Plan: Standardized Testing Genre Study

Overview

It has been well established that standardized tests are here to stay. They are not only part of our school lives but often one of the determining factors that speak to our competitiveness in the job market. Standardized test scores are sometimes the sole representation of a student's level of success in a given classroom, school, district, or state. With these tests having that much weight, that much power, we can no longer simply dismiss them as flawed tools incapable of measuring the potential of the children in our charge. We must instead find ways to help our kids understand and learn to complete them in ways that allow them to demonstrate their greatest potential.

Student Objectives

- Generate a sketch and brief biography of a test maker and use this information to step into the role of test maker and analyze the test, gain a deeper understanding of why the test makers made the decisions they did, and thus be better able to meet the test makers' expectations.

- Combine the subtext strategy with organized inquiry to examine the structure of sample tests and determine why the text is presented as it is and then examine and analyze the test questions.

Instructional Plan

Preparation

Invite kids to reflect on their experiences with standardized tests. (Although you may have to define the term for younger kids, testing is quickly becoming a reality at *every* level.) Invite kids to share their feelings about taking these tests as well as why they think the tests are necessary. This reflection could be done as a subtext: have kids sketch themselves in the center of a large sheet of paper and capture their thoughts, feelings, and speculations about testing in surrounding thought bubbles. (This will be especially helpful later on.) If you are want baseline scores, you can administer a practice test *cold*. The same or a comparable test can then be administered after the genre study to assess the level of student growth.

Instruction and Activities

Session 1: Introduce the Standardized Test Genre Study

1. Invite kids to close their eyes and visualize a test maker, imaging what she or he looks like, the kinds of clothes she or he wears, where she or he works and lives.

2. Have kids sketch the test maker they visualized then create a brief biography of the test maker beneath the sketch. (Generate your own sketch and biography on chart paper as the kids work.) Explain how this test maker will be used to help them understand and analyze a sample test.

3. Talk with kids about how having a better understanding of the structure and contents of standardized tests helps test takers demonstrate their learning more effectively.

4. Introduce kids to the Subtext-Infused Organized Inquiry Chart (SIOIC) graphic organizer (see Appendix C). (This chart should be re-created on bulletin board paper or several sheets of chart paper.)

5. Display the first page of a practice test on an overhead projector.

6. Explain that you are going to demonstrate how to use the SIOIC to analyze the structure of the test. Tell students to watch carefully and be prepared to discuss what they notice when you finish.

7. Thinking aloud, demonstrate one thing you notice about the *structure* of the test—*features* such as title, a direction box, pictures, columns, and so on. Capture this in the first column of the SIOIC.

8. Step into the shoes of your test maker, offering subtext to explain what you as the test maker are thinking—what led you to present this feature as you did. Record this subtext in the second column of the SIOIC. Offer as many ideas as seem reasonable.

9. Move to the next column and name what you have noticed. (Conventional names are not necessary; choose one that is memorable and that aptly describes what you noticed.)

10. Move to the next column and think aloud about where you may have seen the feature before, intentionally connecting it with other aspects of daily learning in your classroom. Record this on the chart.

11. Repeat the process with three or four more features, until you feel kids are catching on.

12. Take time to debrief. Invite kids to talk about things they noticed you doing as you began analyzing the *structure* of the practice test.

If the kids join in, encourage their participation. It means they understand the process.

Session 2: Invite Kids, in Pairs, to Analyze the Structure of a Practice Test

1. Begin by reviewing the work done in Session 1.

2. Tell kids that they will now continue to analyze the structure of the practice test with a partner.

3. Provide each pair with a SIOIC and a copy of a page from a practice test (the same one you used in your demonstration or a comparable one).

4. Circulate around the room as pairs of students analyze the practice test.

5. As a class, discuss what the students have noticed and chart these findings on the enlarged class SIOIC.

6. Ask students to reflect on these findings. Determine whether kids are thinking about the material in deeper ways.

Session 3: Analyze the Contents of a Practice Test

1. Using the same practice test, think aloud about its contents—the genre of the material test takers are being asked to read and, most important, the kinds of questions and answers. Must answers be inferred or can they be found explicitly in the text? Do the answer choices include one that is obviously incorrect? Are more than one of the answers "somewhat true"?

2. Complete each column of the SIOIC as you did before.

3. When kids seem comfortable with what you're doing, invite them to join in.

4. As before, have kids, in pairs, continue to analyze the contents of the test.

5. Come back together and discuss new discoveries.

Session 4: Administer the Practice Test

1. Review the material covered in other sessions.

2. Give each child a clean copy of the analyzed practice test.

3. Have them complete the test. (They will be pleased with how much they know. They may already have discussed some answers with their partner. That's okay. Taking this test is a learning process and a celebration of their hard work.)

4. Debrief. Reiterate the significance of understanding what is being asked of them.

Student Assessment and Reflection

Reflect on how deeply your students are thinking about tests. If you are confident in their growth, administer another practice test comparable to the one used in the study. If you feel further inquiry is necessary, find another sample test and go through the lesson again (or add new features to the chart that's already been generated). There is power in repeated demonstrations.

Lesson Plan: Writing on Demand
Overview

When writing to a prompt, kids are faced with a prescribed or predetermined purpose and audience. Gone is the writer's opportunity to select the message and for whom the piece is generated. As teachers we can prepare kids for this most unnatural form of writing by inviting them to (a) sketch a reader for their piece, (b) use subtext to anticipate the reader's reaction to the piece, (c) sketch the scorer of the piece, (d) generate subtext for the scorer, and (e) use the subtext of both the reader and the scorer to revise the piece.

Student Objectives

- Choose a prompt and draft a response.

- Use the subtext strategy to create imagined readers/scorers and imagine their responses.

- Use this "feedback" about the effectiveness of the writing to identify areas in need of revision and ways to strengthen the piece.

Instructional Plan

Preparation

Students should have used graphic organizers in their daily writing workshops before being asked to apply them to on-demand writing. Also make sure students understand how to decide which prompt option to choose. Make copies (and a transparency) of a well-written prompt and of the subtext thought-bubble sheet.

Instruction and Activities

The lesson has two parts, one dealing with the reader, the other with the scorer.

Part 1: Creating Subtext for the **Reader**

Session 1: Draft a Response to a Prompt and Identify a Reader

1. Tap into students' prior knowledge by asking them to share what they know about:

   a. Choosing a prompt.

   b. Using graphic organizers to draft a response to a writing prompt.

2. Distribute copies of a possible prompt and display it on transparency.

3. Invite kids to watch closely as you demonstrate how you decide which of the options provided you would choose. Emphasize identifying background experience that will help you write an effective response.

4. Ask them to share their observations, and record what they noticed on a chart. (This becomes a helpful reference.)

5. Ask kids to choose one of the options and compose a draft, as you do the same.

6. Return to the prompt you chose and talk about the *reader* that has been assigned within the prompt—the audience for whom the piece is to be written. (A single reader is usually specified for persuasive letters—"You are writing a letter to your friend," for example. A group of readers—"kids from your school"—is usually the audience of a feature article.)

7. On a transparency of a subtext thought-bubble sheet, sketch your reader. *Become that reader*, describing yourself and jotting down important characteristics/information relevant to the topic. (For example, for an article on kindness: "My name is Jake, and I love being a bully. I'm nearly ten years old. I have a few close friends, and I don't really speak to others unless I'm spoken to.") Be sure to highlight the importance of including details that are relevant to the reader's response to the topic. For example, knowing the reader's favorite color would usually be unimportant and therefore not included. However, if the prompt deals with color in some way—oil painting, for example—the reader's favorite color might be important.

8. Distribute the subtext thought-bubble sheets and ask kids to identify the reader(s), or audience, to whom they are expected to write. Next ask them to sketch a specific reader. If the prompt specifies that they write to a friend, ask them to select a real friend and sketch and record characteristics about that person in the middle of their sheet.

9. Students writing a feature article will have multiple readers and will need several thought-bubble sheets. (It's important that kids imagine people who are likely to have contrasting opinions about the topic.)

10. Invite a few students to share their sketches, asking them to assume the identity of their readers as they share their subject, speaking in the reader's voice and thinking from their perspectives. ("*Be* the person. Tell us about yourself.") For those who struggle ("I drew Tom"),

remind them of their identity: "You *are* Tom. Tom, tell us about yourself." Kids need to be so connected with their readers that they can imagine what they are thinking, create their subtext. (This is the perfect time to check for relevant reader qualities.)

Session 2: Create Readers' Subtexts

1. Review what was accomplished in Session 1.

2. With readers (the audience) clearly established, say, "Today, we are going to step inside our readers' heads. We're going to *become* our readers, trying to think and feel what's inside their heads. We're going to write down that thinking—that *subtext*—on our thought-bubble sheets." (You can link *subtext* to *submarines*. Both are beneath the surface.)

3. Use the transparency of your draft to demonstrate how to create subtext for your chosen reader. Reiterate who you are: "I'm Julie, a fifth grader who. . . ." *Become* your reader as you read the piece aloud at the overhead, pausing to think like your reader. When you (as your reader) have a response, indicate the part of the draft you are reacting to. Then write your response in a thought bubble on the projected form. (You might also invite kids to offer responses as your reader.)

4. After a few examples, ask whether kids have any questions. If not, tell them it's time for *them* to become *their* reader. Ask them to reread their drafts, recording their reader's thoughts—their subtext—in the thought bubbles on the handout.

5. As kids work, look for a student who really "gets" the idea. Make a transparency of her or his work, and ask the child to talk about what the reader is thinking. Invite other kids to comment or ask questions, then let kids continue creating their subtext.

Session 3: Revise the Draft for Meaning and Content

1. Share the transparency of your subtext thought-bubble sheet and review with kids your reader's response to your piece. Demonstrate how to use the reader's comments to revise part of your piece, thinking aloud as you work.

2. Ask kids to revisit their original drafts and make the changes suggested by their reader's subtext. (The emphasis is on improving the meaning and clarity of the piece.)

Part 2: Creating a Subtext for the *Scorer*

Session 4: Imagine Scorers, Identify Criteria,
and Revise Draft to Meet Criteria

1. Tell the class, "You have written a response to a prompt. Now, who is going to be reading and scoring your piece? Real people will be looking at your work. Who are they? What do they look like? What is their history? What might they be thinking? Let's think about it with my piece."

2. On a transparency of a subtext thought-bubble sheet, begin to sketch your idea of what a scorer might look like, thinking aloud as you go. Demonstrate "becoming" that scorer as you draw. (*The quality of your drawing is not important.* The kids will accept any representation of a human face. If your drawing is rudimentary, the children may feel more confident about their own attempts.) You can make your scorer cranky or nice, young or old. Tell the children about "yourself" as you work (be authentic): "Let's see, I am a woman, I was a classroom teacher ten years ago, I have an English degree and a masters in education. . . ." Include any relevant details that show your expertise as a scorer.

3. Draw the face of another scorer with slightly different attributes, once again becoming that person, thinking out loud as you work. "Now as this scorer, I am a man. I have three kids of my own who are in elementary school. I'm writing a book on grammar. . . ."

4. Hand out more subtext thought-bubble sheets and ask students to sketch a scorer for their pieces.

5. Ask students to share their sketches and tell about the people they have drawn. Remind them that they are to *become* the scorer, speaking in his or her voice, thinking from his or her perspective.

6. Gather kids together again and say, "Now we know that real people will be looking at your responses, but how will they judge if your piece is good and effective or not?" Some kids will probably remember that a scoring guide is used. Hand out copies of an appropriate scoring guide and discuss the language. Ask them to notice the differences in expectations for the various levels of response. Tell them, "Since I know you will want to be the best, we will focus on the language and criteria for the highest score."

7. Tell kids, "Now that we know what a scorer will be looking for, let's see how my scorer likes what I have written. What is this face thinking as she reads my work?" Begin reading your piece aloud as if you were the person scoring it. Write your thoughts as the scorer in the thought bubbles. Show on the text where something is written that makes you react as the scorer. Point out where the scoring guide supports the evidence you are using in making decisions (or questions the lack of this evidence). (For example, "Oh, I see this writer is using the characteristics of a feature article, so I know this writer knows what a feature article looks like," or, "Ah, I see this writer has given me some data that support what she wants me to know.") Give your piece a score.

8. After a few demonstrations, ask the students to reread their drafts and create subtext for the scorers they have sketched. "Now use your own piece and *be the scorer* as you read it. Give yourself a score as if you were the scorer."

9. When the students are finished, ask them to share their responses with one another.

10. After they feel they can identify why they received the scores they did, ask them to revise their piece once more to make it worthy of the highest rating.

Student Assessment and Reflection

Ask students in grade 3 and above to answer these questions in writing: *What have you learned by creating a subtext for your audience? for your scorer?* Afterward, invite kids to share their responses within the context of a rich discussion about being aware of one's audience and how to ensure that these readers' needs are met.

References

Asch, F. 1994. *The Earth and I.* San Diego: Harcourt Brace.

Allington, R., and P. Cunningham. 2002. *Schools That Work: Where All Children Read and Write.* 2nd ed. Boston: Allyn and Bacon.

Baumann, J. F., and B. S. Bergeron. 1993. Story Map Instruction Using Children's Literature: Effects on First Graders' Comprehension of Central Narrative Elements. *Journal of Reading Behavior,* 25: 407–36.

Berghoff, B. 2001. Going Beyond Words. *Primary Voices K–6,* 9 (4): 34–37.

Berghoff, B., K. Egawa, J. Harste, and B. Hoonan. 2002. *Beyond Reading and Writing: Inquiry, Curriculum, and Multiple Ways of Knowing.* Urbana, IL: NCTE.

Bredekamp, S., and C. Copple. 1997. *Developmentally Appropriate Practice in Early Childhood Programs,* rev. edition. Washington, DC: National Association for the Education of Young Children.

Brown, K. 2001. Reading the world through graphics and print. Presentation at the National Council of Teachers of English Spring Conference, Birmingham, AL.

Bunting, E. 2000. *The Memory String.* New York: Clarion Books.

Cheng, C. 1999. *One Child.* SA Australia: Flinders Park.

Christensen, L. 2000. *Reading, Writing, Rising Up. Teaching About Social Justice and the Power of the Written Word.* Milwaukee, WI: Rethinking Schools.

Clyde, J. A. 1994. Lessons from Douglas: Expanding Our Vision of What It Means to "Know." *Language Arts,* 71 (1): 22–33.

REFERENCES

Clyde, J. A., and M. W. F. Condon. 2000. *Get Real: Bringing Kids' Learning Lives into Your Classroom.* York, ME: Stenhouse.

Coleman, B. 2005. Puzzled About Comprehension and Standardized Testing? Edited by L. Hoyt, *Spotlight on Comprehension: Building a Literacy of Thoughtfulness.* Portsmouth, NH: Heinemann.

Comber, B. 2001. Negotiating Critical Literacies. *School Talk,* 5 (3): 1–2.

Condon, M. W. F., and M. McGuffee. 2001. *Real ePublishing, Really Publishing!* Portsmouth, NH: Heinemann.

Davis, B. J. 2004. Personal communication.

dePaola, T. 1981. *Now One Foot, Now the Other.* New York: Putnam and Sons.

DiCamillo, K. 2000. *Because of Winn-Dixie.* Cambridge, MA: Candlewick.

Donaldson, M. 1978. *Children's Minds.* New York: W. W. Norton.

Dowhower, S. 1999. Supporting a Strategic Stance in the Classroom: A Comprehension Framework for Helping Teachers Help Students to Be Strategic. *The Reading Teacher,* 52 (7): 672–83.

Dozier, C., P. Johnston, and R. Rogers. 2006. *Critical Literacy, Critical Teaching. Tools for Preparing Responsive Teachers.* New York: Teachers College Press.

Eisner, E. 1982. *Cognition and Curriculum. A Basis for Deciding What to Teach.* New York: Longman.

———. 1998. *The Kind of Schools We Need.* Portsmouth, NH: Heinemann.

———. 2003. The Arts and the Creation of Mind. *Language Arts,* 80 (5): 340–44.

Emery, D. 1996. Helping Readers Comprehend Stories from the Characters' Perspectives. *The Reading Teacher,* 49: 534–41.

———. 1994. *Picturing Learning.* Portsmouth, NH: Heinemann.

Ernst, K. 2003. Drawing is thinking. Presentation given at the Annual Convention of the National Council of Teachers of English, San Francisco. CA.

Fleming, V. 1997. *Be Good to Eddie Lee.* New York: Putnam Juvenile.

Fountas, I., and G. Pinnell. 2001. *Guiding Readers and Writers, Grades 3–6.* Portsmouth, NH: Heinemann.

Gallas, K. 1994. *The Languages of Learning.* New York: Teachers College.

Gere, A. R., L. Christenbury, and K. Sassi. 2005. *Writing on Demand. Best Practices and Strategies for Success.* Portsmouth, NH: Heinemann.

Grambling, L. 1995. *Can I Have a Stegosaurus, Mom? Can I? Please?* Mahwah, NJ: BridgeWater Books.

Graves, D. 1994. *A Fresh Look at Writing*. Portsmouth, NH: Heinemann.

Greene, M. 2001. *Variations on a Blue Guitar*. New York: Teachers College.

Harste, J. 2000. Six Points of Departure. Edited by B. Berghoff, K. Egawa, J. Harste, and B. Noonan, *Beyond Reading and Writing. Inquiry, Curriculum, and Multiple Ways of Knowing*. Urbana, IL: NCTE.

Harste, J., K. Short, and C. Burke. 1996. *Creating Classrooms for Authors and Inquirers*. 2nd ed. Portsmouth, NH: Heinemann.

Harste, J. C., V. A. Woodward, and C. L. Burke. 1984. *Language Stories and Literacy Lessons*. Portsmouth, NH: Heinemann.

Harvey, S., and A. Goudvis. 2000. *Strategies That Work: Teaching Comprehension to Enhance Understanding*. York, ME: Stenhouse.

Heller, P. G. 1995. *Drama as a Way of Knowing*. York, ME: Stenhouse.

Henkes, K. 1995. *Julius, the Baby of the World*. New York: Greenwillow.

Hoyt, L. 2005. Comprehending Standardized Tests. Edited by L. Hoyt, *Spotlight on Comprehension: Building a Literacy of Thoughtfulness*. Portsmouth, NH: Heinemann.

Hubbard, R. 1989. *Authors of Pictures, Draughtsmen of Words*. Portsmouth, NH: Heinemann.

———. 1996. *A Workshop of the Possible. Nurturing Children's Creative Development*. York, ME: Stenhouse.

Johnston, P. 1993. Assessment and Literate Development. *The Reading Teacher,* 46 (5): 428–429.

Keene, E. O., and S. Zimmermann. 1997. *Mosaic of Thought: Teaching Comprehension in a Reader's Workshop*. Portsmouth, NH: Heinemann.

Kegan, R. 1982. *The Evolving Self*. Cambridge, MA: Harvard University Press.

Kentucky Department of Education's "Writing Holistic Scoring Guide." 2006.

Kentucky Writing Development Teacher's Handbook. 2001. Frankfort, KY: Kentucky Department of Education.

Koshewa, A. 2001. Multiple Cultures, Multiple Literacies. *Primary Voices K–6,* 9 (4): 27–33.

Leland, C., J. Harste, and K. Huber. 2005. Out of the Box: Critical Literacy in a First-Grade Classroom. *Language Arts,* 82 (5): 257–68.

Lyon, G. E. 2000. *One Lucky Girl*. New York: Dorling Kindersley.

Martens, P. 1996. *I Already Know How to Read*. Portsmouth, NH: Heinemann.

Mills, H., T. O'Keefe, and L. Jennings. 2004. *Looking Closely and Listening Carefully*. Urbana, IL: NCTE.

Moran, K. 2000. Filling in the Holes for Themselves: 6th and 7th Graders Analyze Texts. *Voices from the Middle,* 8 (2): 34–39.

Munsch, R. 1990. *Something Good.* Caledonia, MN: Sagebrush Educational Resources.

Murray, D. 1985. *A Writer Teaches Writing.* 2nd ed. Boston: Houghton Mifflin.

Myers, W. D. 1999. *Monster.* New York: Scholastic.

O'Neill, C. 1990. Drama as a Significant Experience. Edited by N. McCaslin, *Creative Drama in the Classroom.* 5th ed. White Plains, NY: Longman.

Pappas, C. C., B. Z. Kiefer, and L. S. Levstik. 1999. *An Integrated Language Perspective in the Elementary School: An Action Approach.* 3rd ed. New York: Longman.

Penner, L. 1997. *Eating the Plates. A Pilgrim Book of Food.* New York: Random House.

Peterson, R., and M. A. Eeds. 1990. *Grand Conversations.* New York: Scholastic.

Rathman, P. 1991. *Ruby the Copycat.* New York: Scholastic.

Ray, K. W. 1999. *Wondrous Words: Writers and Writing in the Elementary Classroom.* Urbana, IL: NCTE.

Rowe, D. 1994. *Preschoolers as Authors. Literacy Learning in the Social World of the Classroom.* Cresskill, NJ: Hampton Press.

Rowe, D., J. D. Fitch and A. S. Bass. 2003. Toy stories as opportunities for imagination and reflection in writers' workshop. *Language Arts,* 80 (5): 363–374.

Shannon, D. 1998. *No, David!* New York: Scholastic.

Smith, F. 1982. *Writing and the Writer.* New York: Holt, Rinehart, and Winston.

———. 1983. *Essays into Literacy.* Portsmouth, NH: Heinemann.

Smith, J. L., and J. D. Herring. 2001. *Dramatic Literacy: Using Drama and Literature to Teach Middle-Level Content.* Portsmouth, NH: Heinemann.

Solomon, J. 1988. *Signs of Our Times.* Los Angeles: Jeremy Tarcher.

Strange, R. L. 1988. Audience Awareness: When and How Does It Develop? *ERIC Clearinghouse on Reading, English, and Communication Digest,* #29, EDO-CS-88-04.

Suhor, C. 1992. Semiotics and the English Language Arts. *Language Arts,* 69: 228–30.

Tomlinson, C., and C. Eidson. 2003. Differentiation in Practice: A Resource Guide for Differentiating Curriculum, Grades K–5. Alexandria, VA: ASCD.

Van Allsburg, C. 1990. *Just a Dream*. New York: Houghton Mifflin.

Vygotsky, L. 1978. *Mind in Society. The Development of Higher Psychological Processes*. Cambridge, MA: Harvard University Press.

Watson, D., C. Burke, and J. Harste. 1989. *Whole Language: Inquiring Voices*. Toronto, Canada: Scholastic.

Wilhelm, J. 1997. *"You Gotta BE the Book." Teaching Engaged and Reflective Reading with Adolescents*. New York: Teachers College Press.

Wiles, D. 2001. *Freedom Summer*. New York: Simon and Schuster.

Wollman-Bonilla, J. E. 2004. Principled Teaching To(wards) the Test?: Persuasive Writing in Two Classrooms. *Language Arts,* 81 (6): 502–11.

Woodson, J. 2002. *Our Gracie Aunt*. New York: Hyperion Books for Children.

Yatvin, J. 2004. *A Room with a Differentiated View: How to Serve ALL Children as Individual Learners*. Portsmouth, NH: Heinemann.

Index